The Integrated Refugee

A Story

12/07/2020

To IVAN,

A most helpful and
pleasant person to know.
Best Regards

Michael Mircea Colesnic

Published by Michael Mircea Colesnic
Publishing partner: Paragon Publishing, Rothersthorpe
First published 2020
© Michael Mircea Colesnic 2020

ISBN 978-1-78222-735-9

Book design, layout and production management by Into Print
www.intoprint.net
+44 (0)1604 832149

The Integrated Refugee
A Story

Prelude 1975

As a general rule, a refugee loses everything except his original accent. I know it to be a fact from every refugee I have ever met, including from my own experience.

I was a refugee once; over the centuries various strands of my family have always been refugees in some place or another, first around Eastern and Central Europe and now all over the globe. The borders in that part of Europe have moved pretty frequently, depending on the winning side in never-ending conflicts, so much so that the house I was born in, in an Eastern European country that exists no more – let's call it *Oversylvania* – that house has been in four different countries in the last one hundred years, but has never moved a brick! In some respects, I am and I'll always be a refugee but under a different name and guise; different character and values though still the same person.

In reality (in my experience anyway), there is only one type of refugee: a lucky one, a surviving one!

After swimming across the border – a fast flowing Danube – on a cold March night, over to Serbia, trying to escape the horrors of a paranoid communist regime, I made it eventually to Vienna, helped by a young Austrian couple, my age roughly, who were stranded with their old banger having run out of money for petrol. I offered to pay for the petrol in exchange for a lift to Vienna.

My final destination was to be London. At the time I spoke what I thought to be reasonably good English, and I have always had a particular fascination with the English way of being; but there was more. I had always fancied myself an inventor of sorts; I had always questioned the then accepted laws of physics and the prevailing scientific orthodoxy in general. Even as a school pupil I remember one of the teachers proudly declaring "there are fifty billion dollars' worth of undiscovered treasures" and there was I, only ten at the time, politely asking *'If the treasures are undiscovered, who has counted their value Sir?'* – Never got an answer to this question, just some extra homework! Somewhere I had read that out of one hundred greatest inventions no fewer than sixty-two were actually British inventions, and so for me, London became the place to be if you really wanted to make a change; to make yourself a name; to achieve something that would make the world a better place – and with the appropriate rewards for myself, of course!

I avoided the authorities in Vienna – they could have easily sent me back to *Oversylvania*, – and someone bought me a plane ticket to London (for a small fee) and so there was I, a very young, self-declared political refugee, all of a sudden arriving at Heathrow, on a flight from Vienna, with no ID of any sort (it was still possible to fly with no proper ID, believe it or not – if you knew the right people and their tricks).

In my ardent desire for political asylum, I first asked the gentleman who was controlling the queue to grant me the cherished political asylum! He smiled and pointed to a person in a booth who was checking the passports of the incoming passengers. This was 'the moment that changed my life for ever' as the saying goes, only in my case it was more than that. Suddenly, I was extremely detached; it wasn't me the person who was asking for political asylum in Britain, it was someone totally different, someone self-assured, someone determined and most importantly, someone who would protect me and see me through.

The gentleman checking the passports was young, must have been my age, no more than twenty-one, who looked at me with surprise and then, pointing towards a row of comfortable looking chairs, asked me in what sounded to me like a very kind voice to take a seat in the waiting area, mumbling something along the lines of "Sorry sir, but this has never happened to me before so I have to get my boss; would you mind waiting here please?"

And the 'Boss' came and I was taken to a sort of interrogation room and then other people came to talk to me and I spent three days being quizzed in a faraway place in the bowels of Heathrow's Terminal Two, kept in comfortable surroundings but completely isolated. The policy at the time was to detain any would be political refugee for the period his claim was being considered; it was helpful to have some connections with the UK or something similar. As chance would have it, I *did* have something that connected me with this country. A couple of years earlier when I was still in *Oversylvania* I had helped an English gentleman who had been involved in a car crash which resulted in the death of a drunken local soldier who had jumped in front of the Englishman's 'Beetle' in the night. It was clearly a case of an unfortunate traffic accident, but things and justice did not operate according to 'normal' rules in places like *Oversylvania*. The case of a foreigner (and by that I mean a foreigner from a hostile country), who causes the death of a local soldier could well have escalated into a serious diplomatic incident with the British citizen spending a long time in a local jail or worse. Later that night I was summoned by the local police and taken to act as an interpreter for the unfortunate Brit, as I was the only person who spoke some English (self-thought by mainly listening to BBC World news). My English was rather rudimentary at the time but somehow I managed to translate the Englishman's statement, shamelessly embellishing the passages I did not understand in his favour; still, I got his name and address in Britain, somewhere near Barrow-in-Furness. It was like having a premonition or something supernatural intervene. A voice kept telling me, help this guy and your future will be taken care of, and I followed the voice to the end. When the senior local prosecutor went to the toilet during the interview, I followed, and I heard myself saying in a business-like voice:

"Comrade Prosecutor, can this problem be sorted locally?"

To my amazement and sheer disbelief the Comrade Prosecutor, a figure with a dreadful reputation for being a truly beastly character, even by local standards, responded in a quiet voice, almost a whisper: "It can be arranged." After washing his hands, and without saying another word, he wrote on the mirror the sum of money he demanded. I nodded my head, as I was a skilled negotiator, wiped the mirror clean and the net result was that the Englishman was deposited in a local hotel – and even his passport was returned to him. Later he contacted the British embassy in the capital and a representative from the Embassy turned up a few hours later with a small grey envelope which he handed to me eventually, while otherwise completely ignoring me. I resisted the temptation of looking inside the sealed envelope. I just handed it to the prosecutor while watching a football match the next day and the Englishman flew back to the UK two days later and the whole story was 'buried' with the public prosecutor's official verdict: *"No further action required"*.

I repeated this story at Heathrow several times to three different gentlemen, always dressed in the most elegant suits you could imagine. At first they simply did not believe me. However, I had enough details they could verify, and I presume they must have contacted that gentleman from Barrow-in-Furness, who must have confirmed my story. Even now, forty years later, I have not managed to track him down and I wonder at times what on earth he was doing driving late at night on a country road in a remote part of *Oversylvania* – might it have had something to do with the nearby air base where the Russians a few years later were to install their short range nuclear missiles pointing towards the West? Eventually, I would give up trying to find out more about this gentleman, but not yet!

Eventually, a decision was made regarding my political asylum being granted and the smiling young man whom I had initially asked for political asylum, took me and my modest suitcase outside to a bus for Central London, handed me some sort of identity paper with the wrong date of birth (it made me ten years older, but I didn't think it was a good idea to point that out to him at the time) and a piece of paper with the name of the bus station where I was to get off. He wished me luck and said goodbye; he told me his name was Mr Johnson, but I didn't believe him for one second.

I was on my way with five pounds and thirty pence in my pocket … and that's how I arrived in the Royal Borough of Kensington and Chelsea of all places, on Good Friday afternoon, March 1975.

* * *

I found it easy to adapt, to integrate, and to be part of what I love and accept. And sincerely I do love England, Chelsea first and mainly, obviously! In fairness, over the years I was helped enormously by people I didn't know to start with, and who expected nothing in return from me. For me it was extremely easy, I never thought it would be any other way. I've always had a deep desire to integrate into what I consider a superior form of society; who wouldn't in Chelsea? Snob from the start, some would say! Brilliant, but if that means 'being British', let's have lots of it; I've always loved that!

Over the years I have tried to help other political refugees from all over the world as much as I could. I joined Amnesty International and have been in touch with many refugees in which I have tried to instil the necessity of integrating, or at least adapting to the new surroundings, customs and general behaviour. There were happy moments, there were hilarious moments and at times there were deeply distressing ones. I'd like to think that in a way I might have helped a little bit, but on balance, others, people I never knew have helped me a great deal more than I ever did for anybody else.

New Life
Merry, like in Merry Christmas!

I spent the weekend on a drive to improve my English and improve it fast. There was no way I could have done my courses at The Imperial with my standard at that time, so improving my English, and doing it fast was the main action for the foreseeable future. First step, however, was to avoid speaking my native language, mix as much as possible with 'natives' and learn their language and habits, and 'way of being'.

Since my arrival in the UK I had deliberately avoided the small *Oversylvanian* community for strictly pragmatic reasons; they only spoke the native language among themselves; there was little to learn from them and having to re-live memories of my life and my family's near extermination under the communist rule was to be avoided; I had nightmares almost every night, some of them really horrid and the quicker I could get away from all the bad memories chasing me night after night the better: it is still pretty frightening to be chased by Stasi agents every night with impunity and is impossible to describe the enormous relief and the reassuring roar of the almost continuous traffic on the Cromwell Road, in Central London of all places. For most British people I know noise is a pest and something to be avoided at almost all costs, but for me it is the certainty that I am in London and I am *safe!* Besides, I bear in mind a good joke made by refugees about refugees – one finds humour in the most unexpected places! Two refugee couples and their dogs, one with an Alsatian and the other a mongrel, are on a train to the 'promised land' of Germany and are chatting among themselves about their previous life in their homeland. One says to the other: "You know, back home I was a very important person, very rich and influential." The other agrees and elaborates further, "Yes, immensely rich and powerful." While they keep inflating their past, the dogs start chatting too, and eventually the mongrel tells the Alsatian, "You know, back home I was an Alsatian, too!"

In the first few weeks after my arrival I was approached repeatedly by an *Oversylvanian* character, a 'former refugee' who'd been in the UK for many years, so many that he had already found the time to be declared bankrupt twice! He promptly warned me of some of the 'peculiarities' of the British and their total disinterest in the fate of *Oversylvania* and its inevitable liberation from the communist yoke.

"They are more interested in their bloody dog racing than the plight of our people," George (his adopted name) would moan almost incessantly while eating a kebab with fork and knife. He had tried to start some sort of movement for the liberation of *Oversylvania*, but now the movement had split into several factions, although George was carrying on his own 'liberation struggle' with his modest resources. He proudly informed me of his latest 'strike' in the never-ending fight for the liberation of the Mother Country:

"You know, *Oversylvanian* Airways have opened an office in South Kensington just by the tube station? Well, I am the guy that smashed their street window with a brick last week." He told me this in the tone of voice usually reserved for announcements of victorious troops in the last world war. I was not impressed at all and made a strong mental note to avoid him in the future at any cost; my aims were very remote from the 'liberation' of *Oversylvania* and a great deal closer to my personal wellbeing – for the time being at least! Still, I had a last meeting with George who took me to a Chelsea party, pretty close to Cromwell Road and where I met a person that would play a vital role in my next twelve years or so. Her name was Merry, "Merry, like Merry Christmas" as she explained with the most open, honest and beautiful smile I had ever seen. And she was right; everything about her was right and beautiful and somewhat exotic. Nobody had ever smiled at me like that, and from that second I knew that this smile alone had been worth all the efforts and dangers in coming to England.

Laundrette story

A couple of weeks later I ventured to an establishment that had always attracted a great deal of my attention. It is what the locals called a laundrette, a French word for the place to wash – your shorts, shirts and the like. Necessity pushed me every day closer to the door of the laundrette and eventually one Saturday morning I gathered all my laundry, the correct coins I'd saved, put on my best clothes – a decent suit (made in *Oversylvania*, no less!) – and a patterned tie; very proud of the way I looked I entered the laundrette and the world crashed around me: a couple of hippies, no less, were inside the laundrette and what's more, they were using the washing machine and it was clear they would be around for a while. It was the first time I had encountered hippies and I had an instant reaction of almost horror, and I know why. The crimes of the Manson family in Los Angeles, in particular the killing of Sharon Tate, had been big news items in the communist land of *Oversylvania* and the system had blamed the ghastly events on hippies with the net result that everyone – myself included – believed that hippies and everything to do with them was nothing short of evil, and evil of the worst kind.

So there was I, in the laundrette; just me and a couple of hippies. As a rule, I am afraid of people who look and dress differently from me, never mind *real* hippies. They tried to be friendly, said hello or something like that but I pretended not to hear or even notice them; I was busily reading the laundrette instructions and loading all my dirties in the oversized bowl of the machine, much too big for my modest load. After I'd closed the door of the washing machine, I put the exact money in the money dispenser and chose the washing cycle at 'mixed load'. I was ready to press the start switch when suddenly I realised that I'd left out what you might call 'the main ingredient'. I'd forgotten to buy washing powder, and what was worse, I did not have the money to buy any from the automatic dispenser. The very embarrassment and annoyance I felt is hard to describe, when to my surprise and almost disbelief the lady hippie of the pair offered me a full cup of washing powder, refusing to accept any money in exchange and, with such a pleasant smile, even showed me the compartment where to put the washing powder and how to start the washing machine and the dryer. Despite my initial sheer horror at the hippie encounter, after having spent over two hours together in the laundrette making small-talk, I somehow found them interesting, of 'weird' appearance and no doubt dangerous but I considered it better to be on friendly terms.

Slowly, I opened up and we chatted about all sorts. They enquired about my wellbeing, where I was from and how I was managing in London and the like. We had a smoke. I smoked my own standard cigarette bought from a local newsagent, rather pricey (it was my main weekly expenditure) while the hippy couple rolled their own particular tobacco version with a funny smell that made me relaxed and before long I found myself smiling continuously. Eventually, I exposed my limited 'knowledge' about hippies. I'd only been in London a couple of weeks and they were the first 'real hippies' I'd ever met; I mentioned all the propaganda in *Oversylvania* and the hippies had a good laugh at the ignorance of the communist authorities. We discussed my prospects in London and most importantly how to get a good, decent salary for good work.

"No problem, man, there is a very easy way to make money with the minimum of effort," the man assured me.

"How? Please tell me, I'll start now." I jumped at the chance.

"Here is what we do. We'll help you, no problem. It is very simple, here is what you do. First you must advertise what skills you have, or what services you could provide for people to pay you."

"You mean a CV? I have one. I've already taken it to a couple of agencies, but I've heard nothing so far!"

"Oh no man, that is not the way. They will pay you peanuts and exploit you in the process. No way, man, that is not the way; you should be self-employed, work for yourself man and keep all the money you earn."

"Yes, but I have no qualifications yet, and only some work experience in *Oversylvania* and obviously no references, so what can I do?"

The lady hippie intervened with a helpful suggestion.

"You have lots to offer, look at you, you are young, good looking, clean and *white*, lots to offer!"

I was taken aback by the word 'white' but my interest in getting a new source of income was overwhelming and I wanted to hear more.

"Look what we are going to do, we'll help you man," the hippie man stated firmly. "We'll put a notice card in the window of the laundrette," he said, pointing to a small board with a few old notices advertising 'seeking flat' and the like. "Wait, I can do better. I'll write a small advert for you and you watch the offers pour in."

The hippie lady chipped in with her helpful suggestion in making the advert a 'cosmic' success! "Cosmic man, cosmic!"

"You offer your services as a sperm donor and that should do," they both agree.

"Yes, but what is 'sperm'?" My English being rather limited at that time, I'd never encountered the word, but not to worry.

"Well, it is something like being a blood donor, you understand that, yes?"

Oh good, brilliant idea I thought, especially as I had been a blood donor in dear old *Oversylvania*. Just got a meal for my donation there, but apparently you could get money for it here.

Promptly, they both wrote a small advert:

YOUNG, WHITE, HANDSOME MALE OFFERS SPERM DONATION
SERVICES; EXCELLENT PRODUCT, FIRST HAND! PLEASE CONTACT
MICHAEL.

As for 'first hand' that was to reassure the 'punters' that I was healthy, or "something like that" according to both hippies.

I paid the Asian-looking laundrette attendant thirty pence for the privilege of placing my little advert in the window to the delight of the hippie pair who found the whole exercise extremely funny and we parted in the best of terms and a great deal of back slapping; I also got an invitation from them to the Reading festival but that sort of 'music' is not my style, I am more of a Mozart fan, 'man'!

Apparently, the advert was something of a success until someone pointed out to me its real meaning. Luckily, in their excitement and overwhelming desire to help, the hippie couple had forgotten to put my phone number for a contact. Thank God for that!

Working in a pub

I am the worst barman in the history of all worlds; there is no doubt about that! In my defence I can only say that I'd never been in an English Pub before, as I am a teetotaller and I did not know that there were more beers than just blonde and brown as they are back home, or should I say 'former home'? I'm trying to get used to the idea that my life is here in England and all the past is just that, the past never to be repeated despite my regular nightmares where I am being chased by Stasi or Securitate, but somehow I always manage to evade them at the last moment. My future is here and that is all there is.

Still, I had to find more work; so far, I had a job in the place I lived in Cromwell Road, sort of an odd job man. Luckily, I am good at cleaning and small plumbing jobs. It paid no money, but

I felt good about doing something; working a few hours every day and I also helped serving at the tables in the small canteen. The lady in charge of this strange establishment of old people living quietly and content with their fate, Mrs Roberts, was very helpful and suggested I took a part-time job in a pub where she knew the landlord; true to her word she not only arranged for me to see the owner ('landlord' in English vocabulary, a word I have a great deal of respect for!), but she actually drove me to the Nuffield Arms (that's the name of the pub) where I met Mr Marr who smiled pleasantly and offered me the job of a barman just on the say so of Mrs Roberts. I was to start straight away on a rate of one pound fifty an hour. I looked to shake Mr Marr's hand but he looked away somewhat puzzled; later I learned that English people do not shake hands often, well, not at least when employing temporary work, and I was thrown in at the deep end straight away!

I had to clean the tables and I was also in charge of the dish-washer! I had a deep sense of satisfaction and I was already starting to make long-term plans when the pub manager asked me a few days later if I could work every evening. Of course, I'd do every hour the pub required me to do in the evening as it didn't affect my attending the courses at Imperial College. Things looked even better when, two weeks later, Mrs Marr visited the pub in her classic Rolls Royce with personalised number plates, a really impressive sight – and that description applies to them both: Mrs Marr and the classic Rolls Royce.

After the pub manager had had a short chat with Mrs Marr, he summoned me and introduced me to her. Mrs Marr congratulated me along the lines of:

"Oh, so you are Michael, I've heard you work so hard for us and I want to thank you! Are you happy working here?"

I was flabbergasted and left speechless; eventually I managed a few words of gratitude:

"You have given me a job and you pay me every day; I thank you. Thank you very much," I mumble.

"Good," she said in a business-like manner and I departed for my favourite place, next to the dishwasher, very pleased with myself and ready for more good news to come. And here it is: as I'd expected (almost), from tomorrow I would be a barman – well, *assistant* barman actually – on the same money as before, but that hardly mattered. It was the first promotion of any sort in my life and I had an overwhelming feeling of achievement and social success. Since that day I've been privileged, lucky, whatever, I was ready for bigger promotions and great work achievements and this 'promotion', however insignificant in appearance, meant more to me than anything else that I have ever achieved since, later in life. You see, it was the first time I had felt I was accepted; I was part of this glorious place; I was belonging here, and it was with no doubt or hesitation my heaven on earth. Of course, I was still in charge of the dishwasher but as from tomorrow I had extra responsibilities! That was quite a quick promotion taking into account that I'd only seen a dishwasher before in the movies, as nobody I had known back in *Oversylvania* had owned one.

However, it didn't take me long to get accustomed to my new duties and responsibilities, learning fast to identify the several types of beers, Nuffield Arms being a 'free house' and how to give the right change to the various customers who did show a great deal of patience and understanding for my rather peculiar type of 'service'. I could swear that during the many months of working as a barman and being responsible for the dishwasher I had only one unhappy customer, an Irish customer, a 'regular', an old gentleman who took an instant dislike to my efforts of understanding his particular version of the English language until a colleague mentioned the dreaded word, *Guinness!* I did hate pulling pints of Guinness almost as much as I hated the communist system and my feelings were not helped by what I took to be the Irish gentleman's attitude.

Bloody Irish, I thought instinctively, there he is again just being difficult and unpleasant and when he rejected the 'almost full' pint of Guinness pointing towards the incriminating three quarters full pint and mumbling something in his funny accented English, I promptly topped his pint with a good dash of lime! He is still cursing me today for all I know!

Still, there was I behind the shiny bar and in pleasant surroundings; I had my 'own area' and almost all the young-looking girls, some extremely attractive, were queuing to be served by me, and only by me! I wondered how they managed when I took my occasional day off! But, by chance, I discovered many months later that I was meant to ask the younger looking customers for some sort of ID and not to serve 'underage' but somehow nobody had mentioned that little detail to me – it did knock down my vanity a notch or two!

Meanwhile, I managed to get my exams at the Imperial, and I applied for different, well-paid jobs; I was more successful than I expected and moved in better surroundings back in South Kensington where I met Merry. I resigned my barman position at Nuffield Arms and to my amazement and frankly disbelief the pub manager and then Mrs Marr herself asked me, almost begged me, to stay and even offered me more money just to carry on working for them. By that time I was in better touch with the reality around me, the reality that I was a hopeless barman had sunk in – after several months I still couldn't do a decent cocktail of any sort! But I was still mystified how much the owner appreciated me! This question followed me for many years until and one day I got the answer to it.

It makes an interesting post scriptum to this little adventure in my early working British life; after twenty years or so I met this vaguely familiar elegant lady at an art gallery opening in Mayfair, a very glamorous affair, the type you get invited to if you are known as an art collector, which I was, on a small scale to start with, of course! Anyway, this lady, which I had the feeling of having met before, but I couldn't exactly say where or how, approached me and said as a matter of fact:

"Michael, it *is* Michael, isn't it?"

I smiled politely and confirmed it in what I considered my 'elegant manner', a very courteous and gently obliging one!

"Yes, my name is Michael; well, that's the English version of my real name, may I help you in any way?"

"You don't remember me, do you? I am Mrs Marr, we used to work together at Nuffield Arms, remember now?"

Well, that was a surprise. It was actually Mrs Marr; it didn't escape me the elegant way she had phrased it, the bit about working together that is! I recovered quickly, twenty years of life in Chelsea prepares you for 'proper' behaviour even for unexpected social events!

"Of course, what a real pleasure," I enthused with something approaching sincerity. "Would you like a glass of champagne?" adding "*this* time I'll be a better barman" and smiling broadly.

Mrs Marr smiled too in the friendliest manner, accepted the glass of champagne and then we talked a bit about the exhibits for sale, 'pickled sharks' and 'installations', that sort of thing, done by someone called Damian or something, an up and coming artist, not my cup of tea by any stretch of the imagination. After a few more glasses of champagne and small talk I gathered enough courage to ask Mrs Marr the question that had bothered me for so many years.

"Mrs Marr," I said, "when I worked for you as a barman, I was without doubt or hesitation the worst barman that mankind has ever known. I know I was completely hopeless as a barman, as for my social skills I was even worse. Despite all these 'counter qualities' as I call them you wanted me to carry on working for you and you made quite a fuss when I left. Can you tell me why, honestly?"

— 17 —

Mrs Marr took a long, deep sip of champagne while fixing me with her deep green eyes, after which she added as a matter of fact:

"Of course you were useless as a barman, the worst I've ever seen but--"

"But what?" I jumped in anxiously.

"Well, you were the only one of the staff that did not steal or drink during work hours and nobody else dared do that in your presence, *and* you never helped yourself to drinks either and nobody did that either while you were around. If I remember correctly, the takings were at least five per cent higher in the days you worked! It made good business sense to have you around, however hopeless you were at your job!"

Oh dear, what a comedown! I escorted Mrs Marr to her Rolls Royce, new one, same personalised number plate. I kissed her hand goodbye and went to the nearest pub for a strong drink or two. After an hour or so in the taxi, finally back home in Drayton Gardens I relaxed and smiled to myself: there was a good reason to smile as Mrs Marr had not criticised my dishwasher techniques! Perhaps she'd do it next time, but I vowed to do my best to avoid her in the future!

Beauty and being beautiful

Even the most beautiful woman can only give you want she's got, some French writer once wrote; well, he was wrong. A really beautiful woman, like Merry of course, gives you nothing, offers nothing – she is just an icon who asks for nothing while apparently offering everything.

Beautiful women are those women who love beauty but more importantly, *Beauty* itself loves beautiful women. There are phenomenally beautiful women in Chelsea (and I choose my words very carefully!), so much so that I have tears of admiration in my eyes just having a glimpse of some of them (a gentleman never stares at a Chelsea Lady, he just returns a smile if he is lucky enough to be noticed by her). There are so many of them walking: self-assured, distant and totally victorious in beauty and King's Road! (The council should rename it Beauty's Alley, and ban any other women using it during daylight hours, to start with!)

Now I know what Miss Beautiful really looks like. She is one of those phenomenally beautiful Chelsea creatures to be admired in King's Road or Knightsbridge on almost any day; amazing elegance in attire and movement, with features created from a perfect mixture of rainbow and topped with the invisible touch of perfection. Distinctive and unique that is Miss... pure... Chelsea... Beauty.

You'll see a multitude of adverts proclaiming 'The LA Style. The NEW YORK Style, The London Style even, but nobody can buy the *Chelsea style*. Either you are born to it or you have spent a minimum of thirty-five years in the Royal Borough of Kensington and Chelsea, as I have done, to acquire that suave sophistication and self-assured intelligence. Heaven itself must be using the eyes of Chelsea ladies for illuminations at special occasions, I am pretty certain of this one! When in doubt, I'll just start writing poetry – or maybe invent something!

Betting shop story

The South Kensington world got more fascinating by the day, and if I could afford it, the night. Besides the exceptional architecture of The Natural History Museum and The Victoria and Albert Museum (V&A) are the stories behind the buildings themselves. I was told that all exhibits in the V&A are actually donations from well-wishers, mainly locals, but I really found it hard to believe that so many people would donate so much wealth just to have it all in a museum. I still find it quite bewildering and try as I might, it is hard to believe; I'll put this on the 'on balance' tray! Near the top of my 'curiosity list' was a small, discreet setup 'shop', with just a name on it – MECCA – with covered windows and a door with a stern notice warning that only people over 18 were allowed inside, which instantly raised my curiosity a notch. I just had to find out what happened inside this mysterious place a few yards away from South Kensington tube station.

One day I gathered up all my courage and guile and opened the nondescript door, entering a big smoky room, curiously arranged. First, there was a continuous incomprehensible 'commentary' issuing from a set of old speakers that I felt needed proper tuning as I couldn't understand a word. I was aware this was a betting shop but definitely the racing commentary was not English – not for me anyway – which I found rather confusing. How come I had no problems understanding a complex, highly scientific lecture at The Imperial College, but I was unable to understand the commentary on a horse race in a betting shop? And a betting shop in the best part of London at that! After about half an hour or so of just watching the proceedings and listening to groans of despair or screams of satisfaction – *come on my son* seemed to be a favourite – addressing the jockey by his Christian name when winning and '*bastard*' or worse when losing seemed to be the other choice. It was strange to see the way people behaved: everything was reasonably calm and well behaved in between races but things changed to almost a stampede towards the clerks taking the bets a few seconds before the start of each race. The announcement 'under starter's orders' seemed to bring about an extra spurt of energy for the group of punters who scrambled with amazing speed to place their bets shouting 'take price' or something like that in various English accents, while I counted that there were four clerks taking bets and only one who paid out the eventual winners – there were some, now and then!

Still, I had this strange desire to get involved in whatever was going on. I had never gambled in my life before but there was a strong voice in my head pushing me, telling me to get involved, come what may, a voice that I could not resist and instinctively I decided to get involved, come what may. I spotted a rather distant character, who seemed to be immune to all the commotion around him, an elderly gentleman with a cloth cap, cigarette half burned in the corner of his mouth and a crumpled Sporting Life with various markings on each race card. An old boy, I reasoned, the right person to approach when placing your first bet, no doubt. The dialogue between the two of us went a bit like this:

"Excuse me sir," I started timidly, "but what is one meant to do in here?" (meaning in essence 'how do I place a bet?'). The old boy gave me a startled look, looked me up and down for a few seconds and whispered in a strange, melodious English, which I later found out was Irish:

"Get out of here while you can," was the gentleman's firm verbal advice, while simultaneously taking a betting slip and pen and asking me candidly:

"How much do you want to gamble?"

"Well, one pound, no more," I replied, while calculating fast which part of my strict living allowance would have to suffer the inevitable 'cuts', having assumed that my bet would be unlucky! By the way, the word 'cuts' was (and still is) in great demand all over the media, and about every third word on the main evening news – one way or another there were cuts and cuts … and more cuts! And there is still another word that permeates every time an economist is interviewed on TV or radio, and that magic word is *uncertainty* – it strikes me that the economists make an extremely good living from this 'uncertainty' about which they complain non-stop; but more about economists later on. The 'old boy' in the betting shop seemed to be warming to the task of getting a new convert to the gambling fraternity and prompted me:

"Which horse do you fancy?" he asked, showing me a long list of horses with all sorts of coded signs and markings. Eventually, I picked one at random. The 'old boy' nodded his head in approval:

"DEE DEE, good choice, would be there or thereabouts" and he promptly wrote my bet, DEE DEE one pound to win at six to one. I took the bet to one of the tellers, placed the bet, paid the money and felt strangely elated even before the start of the race. I asked my 'tutor':

"So, will I get six pounds if my horse wins?"

"No, you'll get seven pounds," and noticing my puzzled look he explained patiently, "six pounds for the price of six to one and you get your pound back as well."

This explanation settled it and I felt even more elated. I waited full of confidence wondering how to spend my winnings, but unfortunately things don't always go exactly to plan. The race commentary was really something that left me in awe and bewilderment; what sort of English was that? Was there a special jargon just for a race commentary? And to make things worse – and to my complete consternation – halfway through the race a new commentator took over and frankly I couldn't understand a word anymore. Later, much later, I learned that this particular gentleman was a highly regarded commentator and the highest expert on horse racing – shame that I couldn't understand what he was saying, much too fast; a great deal faster than 'my' horse who managed to finish last in any language, Irish accent or not! The old boy who had introduced me to 'the game' would have to answer for it next time I saw him!

Still, I had learned a valuable lesson from my first betting experience. Even now, there are all sorts of English language tests for people newly arrived in the UK and it crossed my mind then that a much more efficient and foolproof system ought to be introduced all over the country. Never mind Cambridge special tests and the like. The best test would be to play commentaries of various racing recordings to those taking the test, and to ask them to transcribe what they hear. Obviously, there would have to be different levels of difficulty and the highest marks would be awarded to those who could make sense of what Irish commentators were saying when in full flow with their two hundred words a minute or so!

Years later, in the early 1980s when I'd already learned – or thought I'd learned – everything there was to know about racing and, most importantly, gambling and the proper jargon and knowledge that only the smartest punters are familiar with, I almost hit the big times when I was within a whisker of winning a Saturday's TOTE jackpot of over one hundred thousand pounds (a sum which in those days could buy you a nice house in South Kensington). 'My' horse, *Walnut Wonder*, I'll always remember this name, was the last on my accumulator. I had already bagged the previous five horses and *Walnut Wonder* was the clear favourite and promptly took a long lead in a two-and-a-half-mile race, looking a 'cert'. I was already spending a good part of my soon to be confirmed winnings in buying a place in Brighton, an old building in Kemptown to be precise, which Merry had loved instantly. With a Zen-like silence and superiority I watched the race take its course and *Walnut Wonder* move further and further ahead of his field of competitors. Yes, there were a few more fences to be jumped but there was a sense of unbreakable certainty that the 'money was in the bank' to use the parlance. This lasted until *Walnut Wonder* met the last fence where the horse and its jockey parted company for reasons better known to everybody else but me. There was no blame to be apportioned to anyone involved, but it hurt, and hurt badly. Personally, I blamed the jockey, this time a lady jockey whose name I shall never mention – forty years of 'Englishness' have taught me something about behaving like a gentleman, if not really being a fully-fledged one! I 'lost' over a hundred thousand pounds but there was a silver lining to this unhappy event. I had been smoking a cigarette at the time and when *Walnut Wonder* lost the race, I decided then and there who the real guilty party was for my misfortune – it was the cigarette I had been smoking at the time. Thoroughly disgusted, I threw it away and strangely I have never again felt the desire or the need for another cigarette, its smoke just leaves me cold, and I've calculated that over the thirty years since I gave up smoking, I have saved more than a hundred thousand pounds in the process without necessarily intending to! You see, yet another lesson in reality and pragmatism!

My colleague Hassan

Sometime before moving in to Merry's flat, while still a student, I shared a flat in South Kensington with a colleague of mine, some-one I shall call Hassan (not his real name), for reasons you'll understand later. Hassan was studying astrophysics, nothing special in that except that he was from Iran. "I am Persian" he would state with the pride of someone knowing they came from one of the oldest and most famous nations on earth, and he was studying very diligently as it happens, a course in astrophysics which, at the highest level, theoretically, teaches someone intelligent enough the principles of how to build a nuclear weapon. At that time, at the end of the 1970s, few, if any, people were thinking that Iran, the main oil supplier and staunch Western ally, would ever contemplate getting involved in nuclear weapons and the like. Thinking back, there were also quite a few Libyan and Iraqis, very bright charac-ters, that at that time, by coincidence or design, were following diligently the same studies – you were most likely to meet them in the library instead of the pub. I saw nothing suspicious at the time. Over time, I became friendly with Hassan who was fascinated by meeting a 'dissident' from a communist country while his own political opinions were pretty left-wing to put it mildly. Among the students there were obviously all sorts of debates, which, if I had taken them seriously, I'd have been better off back in some communist heaven dreamt of, yet again, by incredible intelligent creatures at The Imperial – but sadly not viable in the real world. Well, what a shame!

Hassan, who came from a very rich and old Persian family in Teheran, was a socialist one hundred per cent; for him the Americans without exception were evil. Hassan spent most of his spare time arguing his wish list and absurd points of views – top of the list was the overthrow of the Shah of Persia; second was "getting rid of the Americans" – whatever that meant – and there was always a third aim that kept changing but usually was something on the lines of "extermination of all the rich people" –which he dropped from his wish list when I pointed out that his parents were rich and were paying a great deal of money for his expensive education in London; was he going to have them killed as well? I never got a precise answer to this 'innocent' question which always left Hassan in a state of deep trance, while continuously stroking his very well kept beard. He was in a bit of a conundrum (another long word, you see!) especially after his parents had just bought him a nice two-bedroom flat in Roland Gardens Mews. Hassan, very proud, took me to see it and asked me if I'd like to share the flat with him, rent free, of course. To this day I don't know if he was trying to buy off my ironic questioning or if he just liked my company.

After he got some decent furniture, I bought myself a futon, very fashionable at the time, a table and a chair – all with money borrowed from Hassan on the basis of "I'll pay you back the money when I can". I also, very wisely, invested five pounds, quite a bit of money at the time, in a poster of a melancholic but nonetheless very good-looking revolutionary character, someone called Che Guevara, whom every woman I knew would have loved to have, or simply just kiss. I displayed the poster in my room just above the futon bed and every time a lady 'friend' shall I say, came to visit me, she would enthuse:

"Who is this great looking guy, just look at him?" And I would reply nonchalantly

"Oh, he's my second cousin, on my mother's side, you know."

"Oh, you should introduce me to him when you meet him next time."

Meanwhile my agenda for the day had ended satisfactorily for the parties concerned and I owe a great deal to a chap I never knew, revolutionary or otherwise. Every time I came across a woman I wanted to make love to I'd refer to the actual act as 'The Che Guevara treatment' to the half amused Hassan who could not understand my lack of revolutionary zeal; I would smile and thought that there were still things in my past I'd never mention to anybody at any time. My desire to make love to women was a strange panacea for escaping at times, at least from my nightmares, those of being tortured, that lasted for months and months. Usually they were about myself 'being back', chased by dark figures with no face that were always just about to catch me. At times they became unbearable and I would wake up in the night banging my fists on the walls of the bedroom and cry in unseen pain; it was like a strange power was sending me wave after wave of anxiety and pain which I could not avoid – the reason I slept on a futon for many years, was to sleep on the floor like in a cell, which gave me some sense of safety, strangely. Nothing gave me more satisfaction in the morning than to hear the council refuse lorries early on making the strong, familiar noise that annoyed everybody around but me – that powerful and uniquely reverberating sound of empty bottles from the pub at the end of the mews being unloaded on metal drums was the soothing music that confirmed I was safe in London despite my nightmares – that noise was the very calming panacea I needed every morning.

Meanwhile, Hassam was becoming more and more radicalised so much so that one evening he calmly made an extraordinary suggestion:

"Michael let's go and kill some Americans," he said, and his small, violent, mean eyes were not joking.

There was only one way to reply to my flatmate's extreme proposal to join him in killing some Americans (in central London of all places, for God's sake!) and that was to ridicule his idiotic proposal. I didn't say it straight out, because I couldn't be certain what the guy would do next, so I suggested, in the most relaxed manner, that it might be a better idea to go into Knightsbridge and pick up a couple of girls at The Loose Box – my favourite place – just opposite Harrods, a posh mixture of disco and 'first date'! Hassan must have expected a philosophical discussion on the rights and wrongs of the impending world revolution that would sweep it all away and so was greatly disappointed.

In the beginning I used to have more meaningful chats with Hassan about small things like the future of the universe and the victory of the working class, and the essential bit of Hassan's reasoning was that "you can't make an omelette without breaking eggs" to which my preservation instinct answered before I did. "I can't stand omelettes Hassan, I am allergic to eggs, I'll *never* want a bloody omelette!" – that was partly true, I was not particularly keen on eating eggs for the simple reason that I had no fridge or a proper place to keep eggs. Besides, you always have to cook the damn eggs one way or another and I'd rather have something already cooked; the standard baked beans were more than enough to satisfy my culinary needs at the time, sometimes supplemented by brown bread but not daily – too much of a daily luxury that one!

Hassan lost interest in our discussion as suddenly as he had started it. But this unexpected outburst had put me in a difficult position; what would I have done if Hassan had actually meant it? What if he had really been planning to shoot Americans at random as he had stated? Should I have run to the police and told them about it? Then what? I would have been on the streets, if not worse. I was sharing Hassan's flat costing me nothing; I did not have money for rent and leaving Hassan's flat would have been the end of my studies at The Imperial. As once before in my past when I was faced with a similar conundrum in *Oversylvania*, I went to the Church in search of help and guidance – any church, as long as it had a cross inside that was good enough for me; by chance this time it turned out to be St James's in Piccadilly.

I prayed to God the way a condemned person prays for his life before being executed and asked God to give me another chance, to show me what to do, to guide the way He had done when He had saved me before in *Oversylvania*. I stayed for hours inside the church, frozen to the bench, waiting for a sign, anything to direct me … but nothing came! Eventually, a sensation of warmth and relief overcame me and my mind was suddenly made up. When I returned to the flat I expected to meet Hassan and square things with him. But the flat was empty with a little note for me from Hassan stating: *I'm flying back home tonight to join the revolution. Watch the news. We'll meet again, long live reboltion!* Hassan, in his hurry and excitement, had misspelled the word 'revolution'. The relief, the joy, the overwhelming liberation touched all my senses and I collapsed on the settee and fell into a sort of trance till late the next day. And I woke up with strange pains all over my body and eventually I turned the TV on. On BBC news the main story – the *only* story – was Iran and Iran and more about Iran and the Shah of Iran and his wife leaving the country with the whole family for an unknown destination, to avoid being captured by the Revolutionary Guards. It was an extraordinary experience to watch three thousand years of monarchic rule being wiped out in a matter of hours. I had no feelings for the Shah of Persia one way or another but I couldn't stop thinking about the way the Shah had been abandoned by all his powerful friends in the West and left to die, eventually, in exile, bitter and lonely except for his close family, now themselves refugees. His children would eventually settle in London and wait for the wheels of history to turn again in their favour.

Meanwhile, days passed and I heard nothing from Hassan and with every day passing I imagined him to have made it to Iran to join the huge revolutionary crowds celebrating the Shah's demise and the establishment of an Islamic Republic ruled by Ayatollahs and Revolutionary Guards. I think I saw him once in a news flash from Teheran, when the masked Iranian Revolutionary Guards stormed the American Embassy and took all its personnel as hostages, leading them one by one blindfolded and handcuffed into solitary confinement that would last for years. By chance the camera zoomed in on the covered face of one of the Revolutionary Guards; his eyes were clear to see and they were the mean, malevolent, close-set green eyes that only Hassan had. I had no doubt it was Hassan and my first instinct was to pray for the hostages unfortunate enough to be in the 'care' of Hassan.

Many years later a refugee from the Islamic Republic of Iran told me that Hassan had eventually become a very feared judge with wide powers and no mercy in sentencing to death those unfortunate enough to be brought to justice in from of him. This particular political refugee had been a former judge himself and he told me in detail about the way 'justice' was administered after the Revolution, when like in most revolutions the victors take revenge on the vanquished, but even by those standards Hassan turned out to be merciless and applied just one type of sentence: death by hanging.

"We used to have meetings before the brief trials in front of the Revolutionary Court, look at the list of the accused and decide quickly; there were hundreds of cases every day. There were four of us, three qualified judges, acknowledged as such, and Hassan who was representing the Revolutionary Guards, the real power in the state. We, the judges, would read the list of the accused, the charges and we'd establish a tariff, give this one ten years, give the other twenty years and so on. If there were murderers, they would be sentenced to death, and that was that until Hassan turned up just before the Court started its proceedings and write *to death* in the column marked 'sentence' for the whole list of accused. Hassan only once explained why all had to be sentenced to death – the fact that they had been brought in front of the Court was reason enough; they must be guilty otherwise they wouldn't have been brought to Court. The Court's duty, according to Hassan, was just to pass sentence – death was his judgement, in all cases. It was not Court's job to decide guilt or not, that had already been decided. Why on earth would the Revolution prosecute innocent people? Hassan would insist before losing his temper and threatening us, the judges, with the same punishment. I had to run away," declared this former judge, now an innocuous refugee asking for political asylum in Britain. Never met this former revolutionary judge again and still wonder how the Home Office dealt with this 'tricky case'!

But my thoughts returned to Hassan and in a way, I felt a great sense of relief. At least now he was no longer a threat in Chelsea or Britain at large; he could satisfy his criminal murderous instincts on his own co-nationals, in his own country. They wanted revolution, they got Hassan. This sensation of egotistic relief lasted but a minute as the expression goes. Like most of his student co-nationals, Hassan had been studying astrophysics in London, at PhD level which is generally considered the level where you learn how to make a nuclear device. Most, if not *all* of that knowledge, was now in the possession of the Iranian authorities; what would happen next was the question that troubled me. You cannot *un*-learn something at that level – astrophysics as a science is there at the highest level of human intelligence and knowledge and in my estimation very few people have the skills and qualities to attain PhD level. About six of them were now in Iran working for the Iranian regime, with who knew what aims – and one of them was my former flatmate Hassan, whose philosophy in life was 'you cannot make an omelette without breaking eggs'. This story would not end in 1983, it would go on and on for many decades to come. I just hope nobody is going to break too many eggs any time soon!

Moving in with Merry

Days and weeks and months and interminable debates about the Iranian Revolution passed by without my hearing anything from Hassan. My life was entering a period of quiet routine, with its own excitements and pleasant surprises. My 'liaison' with Merry went from strength to strength mainly due to her boy, Ben, who saw me not only as a very good friend but as some sort of father figure as well. He was a very determined and intelligent boy which pleased me enormously, really. How often do you hear of a ten-year-old boy setting in place house rules with such extraordinary maturity? It made me proud.

After I had spent my first night with Merry, Ben, having been decamped to his grandmother on one pretext or another, came back in the morning and asked Merry straight away:

"Are you having an affair with Michael?" he confronted her, coming straight to the point.

"Well, we are good friends, as you can see, but that is all," she tried to fob him off but Ben was made of stronger stuff and advised his mother what lover she should take. Obviously, I was his preferred candidate; all that skateboarding together in Kensington Gardens was paying good dividends now!

Merry, being the beauty she was, tall, classy, red-haired, beautiful, sexy (have I left anything out? I wonder), had quite a few admirers (about twelve that I knew of!) whom she greatly enjoyed toying with, sleeping with, whatever took her fancy. She was somehow free and reasonably rich – a real catch. And, by the way, she had a wicked sense of humour to top it all. She actually threw a party to which she invited all her twelve 'admirers' and myself, while she was the only woman – it was not the most pleasant party I have ever attended by any stretch of the imagination. It reminds me of another party someone told me about once, a party in which all participants had a stammer except for the host who amused himself greatly! So did Merry, in her own 'artistic' style but the decision who to choose had already been taken by Ben, and that was all that mattered!

"Michael helps me with my homework," was the clincher, believe it or not! Merry, to soften the blow somehow, assured me that I was by far the "best in bed" and things were settled on the terms that I should move into Merry's flat, sleep in the music room and have some sort of semi-conjugal rights, *after* completing Ben's homework and when Ben had gone to sleep in his room. Luckily for both of us we were a pretty good match in bed; luckily, I am well-endowed where it matters, as they say, which is brilliant given Merry's unlimited libido and readiness to make love at any time.

In ten years of living together she refused me just once, the day she kicked me out of her flat. She had a brilliant body and she knew tricks I never knew existed; tricks you wouldn't necessarily associate with a Chelsea Lady! But the more pleasure, whichever way, method or position, the better. There was a slight drawback, though. We had one of the warmest summers in London and we used to go to bed with the windows wide open – and when making love (minimum every night or more often, whichever the greater) Merry would indulge in screams that would make any tennis player blush and, after I moved in, the neighbours began to talk and someone must have mentioned it to Merry. So instead of moaning loudly she would then just bite her lips. A huge fan and a humidifier promptly installed in the bedroom eventually sorted the problem. We then would close the windows and Merry could moan at her sensual bits pleasure for hours and hours, while I was so exhausted in the morning that I could hardly walk in a straight line.

Over time, Merry and I established an unwritten arrangement. Of course we were 'an item', just for her close circle of friends and relatives, a fact met with disbelief by some and bewilderment by Merry's mother. When Merry explained to her mother that I was "some sort of scientist" she asked in her high-pitched and croaky voice:

"What is that? Do we know any other of those 'scientists', whatever they are?"

Merry took her time to explain in a manner as positive as possible

"Well, Michael is very good with science you know and Ben needs someone like a father to help him with schoolwork, and Michael is very good at that, and Ben absolutely adores Michael. I couldn't possibly do for Ben what Michael does, you know I wasn't top of my class at school … well, with homework anyway," Merry concluded with a demure smile!

"Is he making any money?" asked Merry's mother finally, and, after being re-assured that I was making enough money for Merry not to worry about her future and that of Ben, at least for the time being, she gave her grudging approval for the 'liaison' when I heard her advising Merry:

"Keep him in the music room, for appearance's sake at least, and let's hope for the best. So long as Ben is happy and well, that's all that matters." For Merry's mother, Ben, being the only family descendant, was all that mattered, and my accent was overlooked … for the time being!

"Tell Michael to do something about his accent and his table manners," I heard her once whispering to Merry. "He should have learned by now to take food to his mouth and not his mouth to food!" Strangely I found her comment so hilarious I smile even today when I remember it!

The rest of Merry's circle seemed to have accepted me as some sort of useful curiosity that wouldn't last, obviously, but if it was good for Ben, that was all that mattered – Merry could get herself another lover any time if she so pleased. That didn't stop a couple of her closest friends trying to get in bed with me, though. One of them tried it on even in the music room, of all places, while Merry was in the flat! I am not the cheating type mainly because I treasure comfort and cosiness more than any sort of adventure, much too lazy for that. Besides, Merry had all I wanted in a woman, and as the saying goes, even the most attractive woman can only give you what she's got. Merry had the lot, plus a beautiful character, and that mattered most. In fairness I never suspected her of cheating, not even the odd 'give or take a night or two' as a famous song goes!

One way or another, despite our age difference (Merry is almost twenty years older than me, but still extremely beautiful and attractive), despite coming from different backgrounds and spheres of the planet, with so many different values and temptations, we managed to live together without the slightest row for almost ten years, in the blissful, beautiful, gentle world of Chelsea. I carried on working on important contracts in the oil and gas industry, I learned a lot and, importantly, I earned a lot. Enough to be able to go on holiday to Rio at least once a year, carnival time to start with then ventured to more exotic and remote places. What I loved most was to travel to Italy and admire in disbelief its Renaissance treasures; there are so many of them and I greatly envy those who live amongst them – but Chelsea is not so bad either! Merry, having seen most of them before, was an excellent guide and life was sheer bliss by any standards. People do not realise sometimes how important it is to live with someone without ever having a cross word, never an argument, never a dispute – let kindness and understanding rule, was the law of the day, for every single day.

And to crown it all, Ben was developing into some sort of model son and pupil. If not exactly enthusiastic, his school reports were more satisfactory than not, impeccable behaviour starting with the Scouts and very 'appropriate' school friends. As I had no children of my own, my bond with Ben was extraordinarily strong and despite all temptations and traps awaiting any teenager, Ben cautiously avoided every single one of them without me having to impose my will, except for the homework and loud music playing (Heavy Metal and not Mozart, to my despair!). Still, by any standards Ben was the model teenager; all that expensive education seemed to have paid good dividends from a very early stage to Merry's and her mother's relief.

Over ten years, Merry, with all the time in the world, changed from some sort of social butterfly into what she called an 'artist'. She quickly realised she had no talent for painting or other applied arts, except for one that reflected almost perfectly her beauty and character: jewellery and making jewellery. She was in the main a determined woman, and if making jewellery was her talent, she would fulfil it. Almost overnight, one of the spare rooms, quite a few of those in her flat, was converted into a jeweller's workshop with all sorts of paraphernalia to implement a very serious hobby. Quite wisely she decided that silver would be her metal of choice and she soon produced her first 'masterpiece', a phallic-looking crystal in an elaborate clasp which hung from an imposing silver chain which on closer examination was an interesting juxtaposition of my initials. I was extremely impressed and absolutely chuffed. I wore it with pride almost all the time, even in the rush hour on the underground – I bet there are still people around South Kensington tube station who can recall me simply because I wore that mesmeric piece of jewellery. My best memory of Merry!

Political activist

Merry had a brilliant idea. As the election date drew closer why didn't I get involved in local politics, she wondered; according to her there was "lots and lots to learn" from the oldest democracy in the world and I became really excited at the prospect of becoming involved in politics, at local level to start with! Merry's mother had been a long-standing and active tory supporter, obviously, and had become even more enthusiastic when they elected a new Tory leader, a lady called *Mrs Thatcher*, who coincidentally lived a couple of hundred yards from Merry's place (since visiting Trafalgar Square and seeing the original measures established by an English king in the early Middle Ages I had got used to imperial measures!); a lady whom Merry got to know personally when both took their children to play in the gardens of St Luke's Church, just off King's Road.

Merry's mother made a phone call and I made my first contribution to the greatest democracy in the world – licking and sealing envelopes carefully addressed to all people on the electoral register, irrespective of their past voting history or the likelihood of them voting Tory for the first time. Perhaps if we had this data, it would save a great deal of money on postage alone, and after a week or so of 'electioneering' I mentioned it to James, the local campaign coordinator and a prospective MP who replied to my suggestion in such beautifully spoken English, I could only admire:

"Don't worry old boy, we'll win it anyway, win by a country mile," he reassured me.

"But it will save money and we'll be more efficient," I still pleaded my cause.

"Plenty of money, it is all covered by donations and it is also from public funds," James assured me in a paternal manner and with an ever-present smile. I could not help but admire James and almost everything about him was something I wished I could be one day. Everything about him was something to be admired and followed. Amongst other things, I learned from him that a gentleman must have impeccable grooming and shave at least twice a day, morning and evening.

"Look dear boy," he would say with honeyed vowels and impeccable accent, "surely if you shave to go to the office, you'd do the same courtesy when you go to bed with your wife!" He did, however, spoil it later by adding: "Well, wife or whatever, you understand" and he'd laugh loudly. Still, I could not help but admire him, his elegance. He mentioned something about a place called Savile Row and a substantial amount of money for a gentleman to maintain a Chelsea standard of living and to keep up appearances James estimated to be not less than thirty thousand pounds – in 1979! At that time, you could have bought a lovely little mews house for the same amount!

"Is that for life?" I wondered.

"Oh no, that is just for the year and increasing rapidly, damn inflation and all those 'unforeseen expenses' which have to be taken into account," James informed me candidly. At that time, I was being paid a reasonable salary of about eight thousand pounds a year, topped up with a promise of annual increases to keep up with inflation. (This 'inflation' thing was a completely new experience for me, having come from a totalitarian society where prices and salaries were frozen for decades at the lowest possible level. Marxist rules had been applied strictly, but not strictly enough for the 'top leaders'!).

Having got over the first scare that I would never be able to achieve my aim of becoming or looking something like James (minus his accent – *that* I would never really master. Believe it or not, over the years I even resorted to elocution lessons from a National Theatre actor, no less, but somehow, I have never managed to totally get rid of my own accent.) I should have to find a new job, a very well-paid job, and most importantly, I had to carry on with my work of inventing something that would bring me a great deal of money and fame to start with. I am an optimist and very determined, and I was pretty good at this 'determination' thingy! I thought that if I was unable to make something of myself here, I might as well go back to dear old *Oversylvania* and spend the rest of my days in a communist jail or worse – if this was not motivation enough, then life itself was a waste of time!

At the local Conservative Party offices I watched with fascination the way 'dear old ladies' diligently and silently carried on the mind-numbing job of filling in and sealing envelopes with the latest garb of political promises, all of them in blue (both the old ladies and the political 'literature'); also a photograph of a determined looking blonde lady, our future leader, the leader who would make Britain great again and everybody happy, well almost everybody except for the opposition parties, that is to say the hopeless labour party and the 'no chance, waste of time, liberals'. That was our leader Mrs Margaret Thatcher, one of the first women in The House of Commons and soon to be the first woman Prime Minister of the UK.

And 'our leader' won and won well; "joy and happiness galore in The Royal Borough of Kensington and Chelsea", as Merry described it, although she still had her small doubts about Mrs Thatcher but nevertheless Merry joined the celebrations mainly to please her mother and keep up the family harmony, rather than from any deep conviction. James, on the other hand, was happiness itself and a few days later he was promoted to the position of junior minister for his efforts – with greater things to come, no doubt. I had myself this ever-increasing feeling of deep satisfaction and the achievement was overwhelming. On the night of the election I had stayed up all night watching the results arriving on the BBC and I had watched with great delight that weird device called the 'swingometer' that was slowly announcing the results from different constituencies all over the country to confirm Mrs Thatcher's victory. I was still expectant for the next big thing. Not only had I witnessed what for me had been the first free and fair, democratic election, but I had been part of it, I had actually helped to make it happen – how about that! I had only been in the UK for four years and look at that! Surely, much greater things would follow soon!

The team of dedicated Conservatives in Chelsea got a personal visit from Mrs Thatcher and a handwritten letter expressing thanks for the hard work of everybody concerned, which obviously meant me as well. In the Conservative office there was at the time a huge photograph of Mrs Thatcher and James shaking hands with the shiniest smiles you've ever seen. Twelve years later the same James plunged a very deep political knife in Mrs Thatcher's back and ended her political life, "but that's politics, old boy" as he half explained to those ignorant enough to believe in politics!

Merry's mother had not shared my enthusiasm for James, or those like him, and she once dismissed James with a deadly put down, deadly by Chelsea standards that is!

"Oh, he is from a family that buys their own furniture dear boy." She had dismissed James and "his lot' with the gesture of a grande dame you see in a period drama – bit of a shock that comment until I realised that what she meant was that James's family were some sort of nouveau riche, and even worse, very 'riche' indeed – James personally was worth many millions; he was the proud owner of a very profitable publishing company; having found a niche in the market he'd made the best out of it. It did involve a great deal of graft and long working hours as James never tired of 'mentioning' while holding court with his admirers, but that counted for little in the rarefied and aristocratic world of Merry's mother.

Helping others

Without any prompting, I became passionately involved in helping new political refugees in a practical way in their first steps in this marvellous new society where they could say whatever they wanted without fear of reprisal; they could look other people in the eye without cowering their own. Here, where the people in authority asked them nicely and politely what they would like, if they had any special needs, if they had been tortured, if they needed any special treatment, and the like – what an extraordinary country! Bless them all! And I was fully involved in helping with what I called the daily needs.

Most of the political refugees at that time were highly intellectually gifted and well educated; still, coming from a poor third world country into London is more than a cultural shock, it is what I call 'fitting within a behavioural know-how'. What could be simpler than going to a supermarket and choosing the food you require? you may ask. Well, it is much more difficult if you cannot read and understand what the label says. Funnily enough, I encountered the same problem years later when I lived for three months on a remote Japanese island where everything was only in traditional Japanese characters – for weeks I had been buying and using a special bubble bath cream; my skin never felt softer or better and eventually, when I managed to have it translated it turned out to be the 'best' cream – the best cream that is for polishing wooden floors!

Nobody can learn a foreign language overnight and most refugees have greater concerns and problems than learning English fast. In my experience, most of them are very happy for the safety provided by Britain and the tolerance of most of the local population, however hard to explain, but uncertainty about the future is the refugees' main inhibiting factor. This is the constant weight they carry; some till the day they die. It is *complete* integration, strangely, that is the only thing that will set them free within themselves. Every time I make contact with a few refugees, from so many different countries, from all over the world, I try to explain in the most patient manner how they can make their new life a great deal more bearable, and pleasant even. I knew from the beginning not to lecture them, a big mistake made by most politicians; political refugees are sick of being lectured, they want to be heard not lectured. Still, whatever their convictions they must adapt, one way or another, to the British way of life. Learning about the main characteristic of the British, in my view that of being pragmatic, seems to be the best way, well in theory at least.

Reality, as usual, is somewhat different and to integrate you must learn the local rules of behaviour and what I call 'daily living'. I spend as much time as I can spare doing a great deal of supermarket shopping; one of the first duties is to take the newly arrived shopping, irrespective of whatever corner of the world they are from, preferably to the cheapest supermarket – and before you wonder and think 'surely everyone knows how to shop in a supermarket', for someone who has never seen one, or has spent the last dozen years or so in a hell hole of a jail in some remote part of the planet, it is not quite so simple. I remember a particular case with two Middle Eastern refugees; I took them to the supermarket, explained how the system worked, everything went smoothly until I noticed that while one of them was carefully choosing items from the shelves and putting them in the supermarket trolley, the other one, a rather bulky gentleman, was guarding the trolley in a very threatening manner, might as well have worn a tag with *'Don't even think of coming anywhere near my trolley filled with my food'*, and that was *before* the check-out. This true story may sound strange and frankly silly to a person who has never had to fight for his life for daily food, but it made a great deal of sense to those refugees. It took them many weeks to overcome their natural instincts for survival and learn the 'new ways' of this new country, however strange and at times distressful it turned out to be. And before you laugh too loudly, there was myself, speaking reasonable English, coming from Central Europe, classically educated, good enough to become a student at one of the best English Universities, desperate to integrate and everything else … and it still took many weeks with the bus always on the other side of the street. And even now, forty years later, I still find driving on the left-hand side of the road rather confusing at some roundabouts!

As a voluntary translator (I am fluent in a few languages) at times I had to translate the most gory details of torture inflicted by humans on fellow humans; I could see their torture marks, both physical and psychological and every time I thank God almighty and the powers that be for the privilege of being British and being protected by this country, irrespective of what party is in power. And among the stories of torture and despair there are, however, strange moments of what I call thoughtful, meaningful smile.

In 1984, after the dreadful famine in Ethiopia, with the money machine of the Band Aid concert rolling on, some Ethiopian refugees arrived in London and were placed in a decent bed and breakfast hotel near Victoria. As I lived pretty close at the time, I got involved with 'taking care' of them, doing the routine admin tasks like taking them shopping and to the laundrette. As many had never used a laundrette before, especially an unattended one, the tendency was for the poor refugee to fill up the washing machine container with all the washing powder available resulting in a flood and more shockingly, a ban on people of a certain colour or way of dressing. Anyway, this Eritrean group of five was an open and rather cheerful and inquisitive lot, trying to make sense in the main of the news on TV. At that time the airwaves were full of news about the Eritrean famine and everything to do with the poor people caught up in it. This small group of Eritrean refugees were devouring any scrap of relevant information about their native land but some of the reporting left them puzzled, especially one item about the poor locals having had to eat fried locusts as an example of how terrible the famine was, the unfortunate 'natives' having to resort to eating insects to survive! Unfortunately, while the reporter was becoming all emotional, one of the Eritreans pointed out to me that eating fried locusts was a very desirable dish in his tribe, a real delicacy – if cooked properly, of course! Such little misunderstandings though didn't seem to diminish their enthusiasm for watching colour TV, a novelty for all of them, so much so that I couldn't abstain from asking the group

"Great this colour TV, don't you think so?"

"Oh yes," they all but one agreed.

"Have you seen anything more exciting?" I ventured a bit further in my sincere interest.

"No," they all confirmed except for one of them; my curiosity risen, I couldn't stop:

"Oh, yes, what have you seen that's more exciting than colour TV?"

Not trying to offend me, the 'dissident' one tried to avoid a straight answer at first but seeing my real curiosity he explained it to me with a little drawing, an aquarium. He had drawn an aquarium as he didn't know the name of the wonder that had excited him more than colour TV, full of water and with lots of colourful fish. I understood that for a person coming from a land where people die of thirst, where water availability, *any* water, is a matter of survival more important than anything else, to see colourful fish swimming in clean waters was a much bigger attraction than any TV, colour or no colour! I don't remember to this day what particular channel they were watching at the time, but my money is on ITV!

There were hilarious happenings at times. Once a couple from Central Europe hesitantly asked me how they could get their hands on some 'real English tea'. They'd heard so many good things about this miraculous drink, they had even read somewhere that it was the habit of drinking tea that had made Britain the most powerful country in the world in 19th century – there is some truth in this assumption but the scientists point out that it was the habit of drinking boiled water as tea, that protected Britain from the frequent bouts of nation-wide deadly outburst of typhus and diphtheria, which decimated the populations of Europe and Japan and did little to advance development of those countries. In my opinion, the fact that the boiled water came from the pleasure of having a cup of tea, and not from any imposition by the powers that be, reflects one of the essential characteristics of the British people: that of cooperating by consent, accepting, however grudgingly, the edicts of those in power as long as there is the consent of the majority. In a way, this could explain why Britain has not had a revolution since the 17th century; ruling most of the world for over a couple of centuries might have helped!

"Can we have some special English Tea, please?" came the request again.

"But of course, here you are, best of British Tea, grown in China, made in Yorkshire, the best there is." I think I got them PG tips, definitely not Earl Grey, that is my little secret (always mentioned) and, a great pleasure (but just for myself); one of the first of my 'vanity' projects, at least a cup of Earl Grey every day – how much more English can I become?

I got a pack with fifty PG tips bags in it, offered it to the very grateful couple and I left it at that. I met a few weeks later, and enquired:

"How did you find the tea? Did you like it?"

"Well, they were alright, sort of," was the evasive answer.

"Come on, was something wrong with them?" I insisted.

After few more minutes of wriggling, and while I was contemplating writing a strong letter of complaint to the manufacturers, distributors and the supermarket, the unexpected truth emerged.

"You see, Mr Michael," (I love being called Mr Michael, and they know it), "the first three or four cups of tea are OK but after the tea bag has no longer strength or taste so we have to throw it away."

Oh, dear, I thought, perhaps all those adverts on TV were a bit too much for uninitiated! Perhaps a little notice on the box along the lines of use one bag once only might be helpful; it left me wondering how many things that we take for granted are totally bewildering to poor refugees.

Finally, once when shopping with a small group of refugees from an Eastern Asiatic subcontinent, I noticed that they were perplexed by the label of 'buyers' choice' added to several products on the supermarket shelves, especially wines. One of them eventually asked me

"Who is buying the other products, those without 'buyers' choice' label?" he wondered.

I was ready to answer with what I thought was a very witty line, something like "The cleaning contractor, I presume", but on second thoughts I judged that my sense of humour might be misunderstood under the circumstances, and, as they say, I let it pass.

There is a lovely expression in English, a cliché if you want, that goes 'when all is said and done' which should be in the national anthem in my modest opinion, to be borne in mind at all times. I always try to tell the new arrivals that in Britain, the much maligned bureaucracy is much better than in any other country I know or have heard of.

And do remember, you like Europe or your original country but you definitely need to learn to *love* Britain and her local inhabitants, their way of doing things. You'll have to do things grudgingly, of course – just like the 'natives' do!

The fact that your job seeker's allowance is late and your housing benefit has not materialised yet are small, easily dealt with run of the mill inconveniences; they are 'small change' however unpleasant at the time, compared with the fundamental truth that you … and you … and you … and any other refugee already here are *safe*. Safe from arbitrary prosecution or worse, safe to say whatever you feel like, including cursing the people who offer you shelter. But, please, please just stop at words and talk, don't be tempted by anything 'stronger' and everything will be 'just fine'! All changes for good in this country have come through wise words and nothing through mindless criminal action.

Accent

You know you have a perfect English accent if you can pronounce very clearly the word 'quite' in seven different intonations, meaning something different with each of them; and did I try for years and years to achieve just this – and quite frankly, with nothing to show for it! At one time I even 'employed' a good friend, Frank, who happened to be a very talented National Theatre actor, a Shakespearean actor, to coach me into using perfect English, a Queen's English if you please! To paraphrase: never in history has so much money and so much effort been spent for so little result! After dozens of elocution lessons, mainly on Sunday mornings, I ended up with an accent that baffled everyone who met me the first time. Most people thought it was something Mediterranean, Italian mainly, which annoyed me a great deal for some reason. In the end I settled on calling it an 'Austrian accent' with the hilarious result that some conversations went a bit like this:

Oh, you are Austrian, we have a cousin in Sydney, I wonder if you know him; emigrated there many years ago! Most people confused Austria with Australia – it must have been my accent!

Still, I persevered. I gave it one hundred per cent effort as a football manager might say, frankly with very little to show for it. In the end I gave up and I learned other languages instead, hopefully with a proper accent; at the last count there are eight different languages in which I am quite fluent and a few I could get by in, including a strange one: When I worked in Japan for several months on a remote island I thought myself Japanese. By chance, it happened to be a particular version of Japanese, The Language for the Educated Ladies would be a correct translation and if ever I was entertaining it was then I would speak it, trying to impress my Japanese hosts with my 'knowledge' of Japanese. (It does come handy though, sometimes, when to amuse myself, I startle Japanese tourists who ask for directions in perfect English and I reply in the most polite manner in this particular version of Japanese. Quite hilarious at times! Less so though, when back on the remote Japanese island. To satisfy my inquisitive mind one Saturday morning, I joined a queue of people outside the main supermarket, wondering if there was a bargain to be had at some special price. Dressed as usual at my best (Italian silk suit freshly ironed and perfectly polished shoes) I joined the queue attracting curious looks, nothing special, a great deal of people on the island had never seen a real life *gaijin* (foreigner) before. However, things became embarrassing when I discovered that I was in the queue for the Food Bank (free food supplies for the local poor), and the people around me couldn't understand a word I was saying! I promptly bought an expensive and beautifully decorated umbrella that I still have to this day, just to remind me never to embarrass myself again!

Merry, Ben and work

At last I had a real job, a proper job and I got it under very strange and unexpected circumstances. After getting my degree I got a job as a chemical engineer at a multinational company on a rather modest salary for a rather boring office job. I was frankly disappointed but in true pragmatic style I started to look around for 'improvements'. It was 1978 and a period of deep social change in Britain but all I was interested in was my own future and my well-being. I was, frankly, immune to the social turmoil and never-ending strikes in the most unexpected places. I still loved the place and I was looking at putting my 'thank you plan' in action. My master plan, to which I gave – and still give – every day a great deal of thought, would eventually come to fruition but there were so many obstacles to overcome and of course I had the pleasant diversion of having met Merry, an extremely and deeply felt diversion. Merry was extremely beautiful by any standards and looked like a painting of the quintessential English lady: tall, willowy, with peachy fresh skin and sandy blonde hair, always perfectly arranged; frankly, I had never seen such a beautiful woman. Merry was almost twenty years older than me and a great deal more mature than I would ever be. I was really in love with this beautiful creature who was separated from her husband, some sort of writer who had or was having an 'affair' with his secretary, which led to him being booted out from the flat and Merry openly able to show some interest in 'poor me'!

Our 'affair' started slowly but passionately, mainly on my behalf, in the summer of 1997 and without many words but with a strong physical attraction and a great desire in having a 'father figure' for her son, Ben, nine years at the time and confused and unhappy with his family split up. As luck had it, Ben developed almost an instant bond with me and declared me his "best friend", so much so that when Merry, in the early days of our 'relationship' in one of her rare emotional crises (I think Merry was still in love with her husband at this time) decided to finish our 'relationship', to my deepest chagrin, Ben intervened – without my prompting or influence. Even as a nine-year-old boy, he had an extremely strong-willed character and not only did he threaten to leave the house if I didn't return, he actually did just that by abseiling down a drain pipe from the first floor window of his bedroom in the middle of the night with the help of a school fellow from his Westminster school. Luckily, they were quickly spotted by a passing police car and were returned to a completely unaware Merry. The net result was that Ben made it clear that he would run away again unless I was brought back as I was the only friend he really had. And that was that. Net result: Merry declared a sort of 'undying love' for me and I was 'reinstated' in her Drayton Gardens flat, with greater rights. This time I moved from the music room, where I had been squatting more or less on a spare bed, into Merry's bedroom; now that was progress and was I happy. Looking back, I treated Ben more like a younger brother rather than my sort of 'adoptive son'. Ben had a pleasant demeanour, was a keen sportsman and an altogether pleasant young boy in whom at times I saw the childhood I never had! I liked Ben a great deal and I felt so close to him that when I worked temporarily in Scotland, I would take Merry and sometimes Ben alone, to spend time with me in Aberdeen, which he greatly enjoyed.

* * *

I got the job in Aberdeen working for a big American Oil Company, for an almost ridiculous amount of money – this was my first encounter in working for an American company and the way I was hired was bizarre, to say the least. Deciding to get a better job, and most importantly, a very well-paid job, I had applied for a job as a process engineer. Having a degree from one of the best universities worked in my favour and I was granted an interview with a big 'player' in the North Sea oil and gas fields, in full development at the time. While waiting to be seen by the person to interview me, a rather huge and noisy character with a 'funny' accent (whom I later found out was American and the CEO of the Oil Company) passed by, noticed me and we had some sort of dialogue.

"What are you doing here?" the brash gentleman asked me rather aggressively.

"I am here for an interview," I replied, sounding impressed by the gentleman's appearance.

"As what?" he asked me dismissively.

"As a process engineer. I was asked to attend an interview today" and I started fumbling for the interview letter to show to this intimidating gentleman.

The huge gentleman looked me up and down for at least a couple of seconds and then declared with a stentorian voice:

"You are not! I tell you what you are … a *planning* engineer, that's what I need right now … and you are *IT!*"

Without expecting a reply, he took me, more like marched me, to the Human Resources (HR) department where he instructed the head of HR to proceed straight away with all my employment details. He left after adding, "I'll see you next week in Aberdeen." And that was that; half an hour later I was employed as a planning engineer on a ridiculously high salary, plus living allowance, plus expenses, plus travel, plus everything under the sun. I turned up at the Planning Department where I informed the head of the Department (who was completely unaware of my existence) that

I was to start working for him. He found me a desk before rather unhappily going to see Mr Anderson – that was the name of the big brash gentleman who had just hired me without even a formal interview. He came back a few minutes later a great deal more upset than before going to see Mr Anderson and found me something to do, reading about the Fulmar project, an oil platform in the middle of the North sea that I was meant to work on. He regained his smiling attire and looked quite relieved when I informed him about leaving for Aberdeen the following Monday. Clearly, he was not very amused to have me around and did his best to wish me luck in Scotland!

I flew to Aberdeen, the European *capital of oil* at the time, and what an experience it turned out to be! I flew on the same plane as Mr Anderson and watched him being whisked away by his chauffeur-driven limousine while I queued for a long time for a taxi and eventually I made it to the Company offices where surprise, surprise nobody knew anything about my existence. I was kept in a corridor while nobody seemed to be interested in my existence at best whereas some were rather hostile at worst. I tried to make some sense of it all but all I got was "We don't need you, we'd rather have a local person" being the most polite comment ranging up to the first racist remark I had encountered since my arrival in UK. Without any reticence or frankly decency, a couple of people referred to me openly as, "that bloody foreigner, what is *he* doing here?" I was, to use the expression of a comedian I saw on TV (Scottish as it happens) "as welcome as a fart in a space-suit"! Things did change dramatically the moment Mr Anderson appeared, noticed me and promptly asked me why I hadn't joined him in his limousine at the airport. The truth was that I hadn't dared to; he was the Big Chief and I had been brought up to respect authority – and I said so. In the tough world of offshore oil exploration showing such respect impressed Mr Anderson no end, and in no time all formalities were completed and I was installed in a bright new office – to the dismay and open hatred of the 'locals' who, to this day, think that I was Mr Anderson's stooge, which suited me just fine as I needed some support wherever it came from.

I booked myself into the same posh hotel as Mr Anderson and concentrated on doing some work, as I was meant to work twelve hours a day, seven days a week. I found some time in the evening to explore the port area of Aberdeen, also known as the Granite City, as most of its houses and main buildings are made totally of heavy granite blocks dug from a nearby quarry. It gives the town a clean and strong appearance if somewhat morose; the ghastly weather has a great deal of bearing on this; – unfortunately, the morose air and deep unfriendly suspicion seem to reflect in the locals' character and behaviour so much so that I had a bet with a colleague on the lines of "you'll never see a sober Scotsman smiling openly to a stranger" – I won the bet more than once!

I had to adapt to the local conditions, after all I would be spending a great deal of time working with the Caledonian 'friends'. I was in 'their' country and quite aware of it. Wisely or otherwise, I decided that it should be me the one who would take the first step towards an atmosphere of 'friendship and understanding' with the 'natives' … and where better to start than in one of the well-established pubs in the Aberdeen harbour. I walked into the first one in the harbour, a rather dark saloon with customers quietly nursing whatever they were drinking, except for a couple of nondescript age who were having what I took to be a quarrel, and an ugly one by Chelsea standards; later I was to find out that it was just some friendly banter – by local standards that is! I went straight to the bar, being an expert by now in drinks and cocktails and the like and I calmly ordered in an assured, pleasant manner, the way one does in King's Road:

"Large Baccardi and Coke please, lots of ice, no lemon."

I swear, the guy sitting on a tall chair at the bar fell on the floor and, resorting entirely on the most popular Gaelic word, the one that starts with f and ends in k, expressed his deepest disgust for me and whatever I was going to drink. The barman seemed unmoved, so I repeated in the sweetest manner, my original request. Accentuating the word 'large' seemed to mollify him and the atmosphere relaxed greatly after I offered to buy a drink for the gentleman who had fallen earlier from his chair; which he 'accepted' with the grace of a drunken sailor together with another curse directed not only at myself but the whole of mankind at large and a bit more besides! Anyway, after yet another couple of drinks, courtesy of my company expenses, he became completely mollified but kept swearing, I presume just to keep the old habit going; he seemed to feel much safer that way! Then I was joined at the bar by what I had thought was the quarrelling couple and, after being given the honour of buying them a couple of large whiskies, they reassured me that there was no such thing as foreign people, "just friends you've never met before" – preferably *generous* friends you've never met before. Altogether my visit to a pub with 'local colour' proved to be a rather funny and enlightening experience; at times I have fond memories of it, but I never went back there and I don't think I'll do so anytime soon! As for drinking in Caledonian pubs, when I worked in Peterhead (that's Aberdeen's ugly sister!) I did the same pub routine more or less but that was quite enough. The second time I went to the same, in the harbour (where else?) someone took a great dislike to me, my person and almost everything else. He became very aggressive towards me and after the usual display of local vocabulary, all eight words, all starting and finishing in 'f', he eventually shouted:

"Outside!"

"You what?" I replied, totally unconcerned and wondering why on earth he would want to go outside on such a dreadful, windy, rainy November evening.

"OUTSIDE!" he insisted almost screaming, *"COME OUTSIDE!"*

"No chance," I replied, "it's raining outside; here, let me get you a drink, what you having?"

Suddenly, the prospect of going outside didn't look that attractive anymore to my new Caledonian friend. He grudgingly accepted a double whisky after which he fell asleep half slumped on the floor.

"Is there something wrong with him?" I asked the barman.

"Oh no, he always does that with every new Sassenach, always ends up getting a drink or two. You've been done," the barman laughed loudly, after which he made a chalk mark on a table by the bar. There were at least another dozen chalk marks on the table and it was only Tuesday evening!

In fairness I must say that generally the 'natives' are less aggressive than the first impression might suggest; thinking back, the greatest insult I ever had to endure in Bonny land was one shouted by the young 'natives', that of

"Oi, you Englishman" they would shout, accompanied by the inevitable version of the f-word. One evening I was met by two 'guys' who were very determined to mug me if not worse. It was on a dark street late at night and it did not look good; my choices and chances looked rather limited. After the customary 'who the fuck're you?', one of them pointed to my elegant black Borsalino hat and enquired, advancing aggressively:

"Who the fuck're you, the fuckin' Godfather?"

Without thinking I found myself answering in kind

"I'm with the fuckin' Soprano family and if you touch me they will come after you and your fuckin' family. You've seen them on the telly, they are my cousins!"

I have never seen someone disappearing so fast in my life. It was like they never existed, and I made a mental note to send a letter to the director of the Sopranos drama series and tell this true story. But somehow, I've never managed to write it!

* * *

Still, working in Aberdeen and the offshore trips, awarded me a ridiculous amount of money; I and a few of my colleagues were on such high rates that one day I discovered to my sheer bafflement that I was being paid more than the Prime Minister, believe it or not! And all that from sheer hard engineering work, nothing of the speculating in the City, financial fraudulent behaviour and the like – everything was from the honest work of extracting oil, an extremely precious product. Mind you, our excuse was "We might be paid more than the Prime Minister, but we don't do as much damage as the Prime Minister does!" On top of that I was being paid additional money as 'living expenses', so much so that I felt able to invite Merry to come and a have a taste of Aberdeen as she had a rather high opinion of the Caledonian lot. In Drayton Gardens only two foreign accents were deemed acceptable to Merry's mother – one of them was mine (temporarily, that is, and not having much choice in the matter) and the other one was a Scottish one! Merry was too polite and in true Chelsea Lady style declared Aberdeen "interesting". She spent most of the day on a windy and rain swept harbour, among tugs and supply ships. The net result was that she got soaking wet with her hair "an absolute mess" after a prolonged encounter with the 'gentle' winter Aberdeen breeze. She had to try the 'best' local hairdresser, with what I'd call mixed results which I enthused about, but I don't think Merry believed much of it. She also decided that it was much better for me to fly to London than for her to visit Aberdeen, every two weeks or so – oh well, some people are never satisfied!

Working offshore, two weeks on, two weeks off brought me not only a great deal of money but a great deal of free time. I quickly found a solution how to spend the spare time on the platform offshore and benefit greatly from it. The time I describe is the early 1980s, long before internet gambling was even heard of. It did not take me long to discover that I could use all the spare time I had on the platform offshore, given the excellent engineering and construction standards; there was little for me to do except stare at the sea and the migrating birds. I couldn't concentrate deeply enough to come up with the new ideas for the great invention that I was ultimately to come up with one day! Meanwhile, the idea of opening some sort of 'betting shop' on a platform appeared to be not such a bad idea after all! There were nearly two hundred people at any one time on the platform, with nothing to do in the evening, except to watch movies or Norwegian TV, the only channel available. Oh, how I laughed at and ridiculed that incompressible language and those endless programmes about how to boil eggs, cook swedes or carrots, sometimes even cabbage – the highlight for a Saturday evening TV. Little did I think that one day British TV, the best in the world no doubt, if you listen to their own blurb, would one day saturate the airwaves with endless cooking shows – cooking almost anything. I'm looking forward to a programme that shows you how to cook your shoes with a different flavour for each! Still, boredom proves stimulating at times; many great ideas have their roots in a period of mind-boggling boredom!

There is zero tolerance of drinking on offshore platforms; there is no social life as such, and the second half of a two-week stint is at times almost unbearable. Monotonous repetitive tasks are not designed for human beings in my opinion, let the machines do that. Sounds great but the reality is different and going on the principle that 'I'd rather light a candle than curse the dark' I came up with the simple and brilliant idea of organising some sort of betting shop on a platform, all very quiet obviously, just a friendly bet between friends, nothing official or blatantly open, just something to pass the time and make people relax and work harder! We never talked about success or good luck – that was me and my little 'private' enterprise.

I started modestly with just a few 'bears' interested – *bears* was the nickname for the guys who did the real hard tasks offshore, the electricians, pipers, welders and the like – but word spread and as luck would have it, the Grand National was the next big one. The net result was that a 50/1 outsider won the race and the other thirty-nine horses were losers. For a bookmaker it is impossible to lose, even if I had tried, which was not the object of the exercise to start with! Even better, more and more outsiders kept winning the important races of the calendar. I remember well a horse called *Roland Gardens*, the name of the street next to Drayton Gardens, that came in at 28/1 in the two thousand Guineas race of the year; The Derby was won by a 33/1 outsider as well. The net result of all this was that I was making more money from my little gambling venture than I was paid for my daily job. Of course, I never bothered to explain to my faithful punters in detail that in a race with forty horses, there would only be one winner. Better still in a golf tournament, the real big 'steamers', that is before Tiger Woods turned up and won everything for a decade or so. There were one hundred players but only one winner – *me*, as a rule! Strange as it might sound I never had even one unhappy customer. The 'bears', especially those of Scottish origin, were very fond of slow horses and I don't have it in me to spoil their enjoyment with boring details as form, previous results and the like. The only problem I encountered was transporting all that cash at the end of every alternate fortnight shift; how on earth was I to explain coming back from the offshore platforms with a great deal more cash than I had started with? But luckily, my famous luck held me in good stead as the body checks were designed mainly for people travelling *to* offshore platforms than for those returning from them. But all good things come to an end, even my luck at times, and it came in a less expected manner that I had envisaged.

Flying in and out to North Sea oil and gas platforms is a hazardous and dangerous enterprise, especially in bad weather – and there is plenty of unexpected bad weather in this famous stretch of water; when flying in bad weather in the big, noisy, twin choppers kitted in a 'survival suit' you are practically blind and deaf. On my last trip offshore, on the return flight something went wrong. We could hear the deafening noise of the twin rotors, but we did not seem to be moving forward. A few minutes later we noticed water seeping up through the floor. It was clear to everyone that we had ditched in the water in the middle of the North Sea and most likely we were going to drown. It was late at night; there would be no meaningful rescue efforts until the morning and perhaps this was to be the end – but not the end I had envisaged. No, this was not going to happen and I immersed myself in the deepest, most sincere prayer I was capable of and, in desperation, I promised God and everyone else that I would never tempt fate or their patience by venturing again in flying over the North Sea. I will never know if it was the depth of my prayer and the promise I made, or the skill of the flying crew in restarting the engines and somehow pulling up the helicopter the vital few feet above the water before somehow managing to land it half an hour later at Dice heliport. I recall that returning crews are usually a very joyous crowd and almost everybody makes it to the airport pub for the much missed alcohol, in its many forms and guises, but this time everyone was quiet and very much alone with their thoughts and worries. Having been so very close to death, and what would have been an extremely painful one – drowning in the cold waters of the North Sea is considered so painful that the fishermen there are said not to learn to swim so that the ending will be swift, a few minutes at most, should they fall into the icy waters. All these thoughts made the decision for me; never again would I board a chopper and fly to an oil platform, whatever money or other rewards offered. My ancestors in their wisdom came with a valid expression I had better always bear in mind: *Everything is negotiable, but death.* Especially a very painful one!

But my luck was holding up well and things kept turning in my favour, so much so that with the experience I had gained in the North Sea I was in great demand as an oil and gas consultant. I learned a great deal from Shell Expro, especially on the practicality of implementing a project on time and budget in an exceptionally hard environment, and I saw what proper capitalism in practice can do when it really wants to achieve something, even it means literally to throw money at it; that is what the oil companies did and they got exceptional results far ahead of the other industries in the country. It was working for the much maligned oil and gas exploring industry that I learned how to put a project together and more importantly, I learned how to produce a realistic project control system that would make sure the project was completed on time and within the allocated budget. I became so good at producing just this sort of project control system that in 1988 when The Channel Tunnel Project ran into so many difficulties, that the banks were threatening 'to pull the plug' on the whole project, I was called in and within two months I had produced a project control system that gave the interested parties a workable plan with realistic dates and most importantly, a properly budgeted amount of money. Everybody bought into the new project control system and in time it transformed the project into the technical and commercial success it is today. In fairness, all I did was to apply to a civil project the latest project control advances I had learned from Shell. And it worked brilliantly. And just to complete my defence of the exploration oil and gas companies – not to be confused with the trading arms of the same companies – when you moan about paying more than a pound or so for a litre of petrol, consider that the petrol has had to be extracted, transported, refined, delivered, not to mention all the stages of the selling chain, while you cheerfully pay twice as much for a litre of 'mineral' water with a fancy label on it!

Just thirteen years after arriving in Britain practically destitute and with hardly any superior form of education, I was the guy who had produced the Operating Plan for one of the greatest civil engineering projects in the world – well that's not bad. But what was to come? What was the next 'trick'? What do you do for an encore but a much bigger and better one, if that was at all possible? Where was the discovery, the invention that would revolutionise everything on earth? Surely it was only a matter of time for someone like me to come up with just that. Free energy for all, anywhere in the world, but remaining the property of the British people, of course! Meanwhile, I had some other pressing things to deal with.

Wembley football match

There was a great deal of emotional reactions on display in the country, recklessly stoked by some irresponsible media outlets, to use a proper expression, regarding the 'enormous flood of refugees' that threatened 'to swamp the country' at any moment. It was 1981 and I was caught between two main currents of opinion. One that said that immigration must be stopped immediately for almost everyone that had no business being here, espoused by the Tory government led by this formidable lady called Mrs Thatcher, and 'the alternative', the one strongly advocated by the Opposition, the 'everyone can come, refugees welcome' brigade. I followed the debate closely but was somewhat detached as I considered that it wouldn't affect me in the least, that was until the Government decided for the first time to send a refugee back, a would be political refugee from a communist country – and a white one to boot. This seemed to be a complete departure from previous policies, and it was a bit of a shock to the system.

I had become a member of Amnesty International during the previous two years, something I kept quiet from Merry, although in fairness she was totally unbiased in the matter of equality and race relations – most likely inherited from her 'unofficial father' a bohemian painter of some repute, long since dead and some say of Jewish origin; Merry seemed to have inherited quite a bit from him, but definitely not his painting skills. And there was something else that I encountered almost every day in the attitude and behaviour of people around me at that time, something that you never encountered in a dictatorial regime: something called *tolerance*. Generally, the British people are extraordinarily tolerant and understanding towards newcomers, and this attitude goes to extraordinary lengths at times. I used to be flabbergasted by well publicised cases like that of a Sikh gentleman who would not wear a helmet while driving a motorbike because his religion prohibited him from wearing anything over the traditional turban worn by the followers of the Sikh religion. He won his case in Court and I wondered how long before someone like me, coming from a country with right-hand drive, would insist on doing the same in Britain, where everyone drives on the left! That would be a tricky one for the House of Lords to decide, I bet! Over the years I started to spot those with real grievances and those (a big majority) that were out just for personal advantage with little concern for the rest!

As it happened, racial tension was very high in 1981; there had been rioting again in places like Brixton, in South London (poverty and criminality being the main reasons, depending on who you listened to or what newspaper you read) but nothing of the sort in the Royal Borough of Chelsea, thank God!

It is strange to see how London has developed over the centuries into quasi-independent boroughs, over 30 of them at the last count. And hardly any two of them have the same interests or aims – that is why London never had a revolution like Paris or other European capitals, as Merry never tired of explaining. If the expression 'location, location, location' is to be believed, then London is the best example – there are streets where one side belongs to a particular borough and the opposite side belongs to a different one, identical houses or flats on both sides, different prices … frankly, I find this bizarre but there we are! Still, having what some people call 'race riots' was, and still is, unsettling, as was the intervention of some of the politicians in power at that time.

One of the ministers asked a very pertinent question to my mind, that of asking Pakistani immigrants and their descendants in the UK, altogether numbering a few million some said, whom they would support in a cricket match between England and Pakistan. Would they support their adopted country, England, or would they support their country of origin, Pakistan? The very question created a great big row and one rather direct politician was subjected to a great deal of verbal abuse; but the politician stuck to his guns and the dispute festered on. While I was contemplating my own attitude to this question, I had to face it personally. By coincidence, at the same time, *Oversylvania's* football team had been scheduled to play England at Wembley in a vital match in the qualifications for the European Championship. I mulled over the questions, who do I support in this particular case, who am I going to cheer on, *Oversylvania*, the country I was born in or England, the country that was making me what I am?

During my appalling childhood, when my father was killed by the communist regime and my mother thrown in jail for attacking the judge who had sentenced my father, I was left to my own devices for years, helped only by the nearby gypsies and secretly by a few other kind people. I was only eleven years old and I was completely ostracised by most of the other children at school. The only escape I had was sport, I just happened to have a real talent as a goalkeeper. I was never afraid of the ball, somehow it never hurt me or scared me; a possible explanation could be that after what I had been through and the nature of the society I was living in, being hit by a ball was a 'doddle'. I was lucky to have had a trainer that greatly improved my natural talent and I was so good that I ended up being selected for the country's junior team – that was till a comrade objected to the son of a 'country traitor' representing the national team, and that was that. Still, performance sport turned out to be a beautiful time for me, a time when I could escape the day to day realities and I still have fond memories of it. A couple of my former team mates went on to be *Oversylvanian* players, and I went to meet them once, just to say hello and perhaps show off a bit!

'Who would you cheer on?' asked Merry candidly, although the question was much more serious than it looked. She knew my past very well, also she knew my passion for sport, but her question had a deeper meaning; at times, very rarely, she would ask strangely meaningful questions under the guise of a throwaway remark when she would try to penetrate my sincere feelings – she sensed that there were still hidden parts in me that she wanted to know more about.

I adopted a sporting approach to her question – as a goalkeeper I learned that there was no hiding place, there was no place for mistakes either, and above all, you had to be open and truthful – and I was just that.

"Look," I said, "I'd like *Oversylvania* to play well but England to win as they badly need the points" as that reflected my true feelings at the time. Merry seemed delighted with my considerate response. As it happened, the match, attended by myself and Merry and Ben in the executive lounge, ended in a draw despite Ben cheering non-stop for *Oversylvania*, just to make a bit of mischief and something to tell his mates at his Westminster school; otherwise not much was heard about football and the like in Merry's household.

Being witty

They will even buy you a drink in the pub and then you know you've arrived! You are almost an adopted son. Spend your time thinking of some sort of witty remark. One such example that helped me a great deal in Scotland was my remark to a happily cursing Scottish colleague who was effing and blinding (a bit of a favourite pastime for the Caledonian lot). Within earshot of everybody else I said:

"You see, the English language is the richest language on earth, over two hundred thousand words, and you are still stuck on the first two dozen or so!" It got me a round of applause and more 'street cred' than any of my 'posh' qualifications. To those of a less sophisticated nature I'd point out that hair washing or having a shower was not just for Christmas, it was perfectly legal to do it every day

By the way, another of my witty remarks to be used strictly 'north of the border' was the one I had in reserve for the drunken 'lassies' who, for reasons best known to themselves, when drunk, which was strictly compulsory in Aberdeen's pubs after seven pm during the week and at all times over the weekend!, would show an extraordinary interest in my red Borsalino hat! "Quite touching too" was invented for them. A few seconds later, the most enterprising lass would make a perfect dive to grab my hat, accompanied by the ever so musical "give me that" in a perfect, much admired Highlands accent, or something close to it. My expensive Borsalino hats I insisted on wearing all the time anywhere in the UK were in their greatest danger in the Granite City – Aberdeen.

"Give me that!" the drunken lassie would insist with a determination inherited, no doubt, from the great Robert the Bruce or someone of similar status, and a determination fuelled by the eighty per cent proof alcohol, if their breath was something to go by. As a rule, most of the lassies were fat, there is no other word for it, and of undetermined age, thirty plus VAT, of course; none of them had been cursed with charisma, must be something to do with the weather – that's ghastly too! What a perfect combination! In fairness it must be said that the men were not exactly Christmas presents either – most of them were cursed with negative charisma! As for the way they dressed, you would never believe how much could be done with cheap plastic! They wore so much plastic that I swear they were a real environmental hazard!

One thing stood me in good stead (just learned this one!), and that was humour. I find it so easy to put people down using humour knowing perfectly well that they are unable to retort with humour – brilliant!

In a word, or more, I was not in Aberdeen on a cultural exchange by any stretch of imagination, but I did make quite a bit of money. So much so that by 1984 I was able to comfortably return to my beloved Chelsea and spend all my time with Merry and Ben. London and more so Chelsea seemed to be in a non-stop campaign for sorting all the world's ills by making money, *lots* of money; the unashamed boast of everyone including myself. Eating, I started putting on weight to Merry's disapproval, and partying, to everyone's approval! Ron and I got much closer; Ron was divorcing Zeta, but this was hardly news as everybody seemed to be divorcing everybody else to the despair of Robin, the choreographer with royal connections (well, he danced once with Princess Diana at a charity ball of some sort, not that he would ever have mentioned her name, God forbid!)

"Why are they all divorcing" Robin would wail in the most dramatically correct manner, "and *I* cannot get married to the person I *love*?" Everyone knew that Robin was gay – that mattered not an iota in Chelsea. Of course, everyone knew that the marriage he wanted was not yet legal in England but over the years things went Robin's way, but I never knew if he ever got married. He always came alone to Merry's parties, strange that one!

Ron, who didn't make a secret of the fact that he fancied them young, around twenty was his favourite age, and very slim, once brought someone who had the requisite 'bedroom eyes' and who wore very sexy, 'fuck me' shoes as my Caledonian friends would have said, was introduced as Ron's personal assistant. To me she looked like someone you are attracted to not for her mind but for the things she doesn't mind!

Altogether the parties were in full swing all over Chelsea and everybody tried to go that bit better, but not flashier, it wasn't the done thing in Chelsea. To be a 'native' of Chelsea meant going back at least six generations – and I met personally at least four families that would have creditable claim to the throne no less. The men were more interested in making money in the City! Whatever Mrs Thatcher and her Chancellor of the Exchequer did, it seemed to work, well, it actually did work superbly to everybody's merriment and satisfaction. It seemed that all the world's ills could be easily sorted by eating, drinking and partying, though not necessarily in that order.

At parties I met a new 'class' of people, brash, very well dressed but not quite Savile Row standard (is it the cloth that wears them or they who wear the suit?) They worked in the City mainly, they were very well groomed, and some had 'funny' accents, but then my accent at that time was not Mozart's music either! They were 'Maggie's children' as they proudly proclaimed but they were brash and lacked class as Ron used to say; he hated this new young intake of hunter/gatherers with slapping smiles and I was not exactly their greatest fan either, especially when some of this misguided new breed of 'guest' tried their luck with Merry – it was just not the done thing at Merry's parties!

Still, there was always something to see and to learn. To my amazement one of the most intelligent answers I ever heard did not come from a famous contemporary wit, but from a beautiful woman, a former model (almost all drop dead gorgeous girls I met – and still meet – at Chelsea parties were former models, whatever that means). This particular lady, an exceptionally good-looking and charming creature, had recently married one of the richest men in the country; they seemed to be a happy couple (Chelsea speak for 'no public scandal' for all I know), but I never met the guy, he was never around (too busy making money no doubt) and there was a bit of whispering behind his back but I doubt he cared much about it. However, at one of the more raucous parties, a well-known TV presenter, more of an autocue reader than the 'real thing', having had the proverbial *too much to drink* decided to have a go at Marlyse, that was the lady's name, and in an unwise move asked her loudly:

"You would have never married your husband if he were not a multi-millionaire, a billionaire perhaps, would you?" He pointed triumphantly.

I froze and was ready to jump to Marlyse's defence, but the lady needed no defence. She turned out to be more than a match for the TV personality! By the way, as a rule, in Britain, if everything else fails, you have no particular skill, no talent whatsoever, don't despair … you can always become a TV personality. Anybody can be a reality TV personality! Sorted!

Marlyse knew that the best answer to a question was obviously another question, especially to a drunken non-entity.

"Do you think my husband would have married me if I were not beautiful?"

Returned to sender, and that was that. I was truly impressed and made a mental note to remember it, using versions of it as my own contribution to civilisation – just joking.

IRA bombing campaign

As a newcomer I knew little about the turbulent story over centuries of the English and Irish, the confused historical past, vague ideas of the rights and wrongs of both parties, but what I knew for certain was that England was right and Ireland definitely not! My passion for everything British (Britain and England were more or less the same thing for me at the time) and I had many fiery arguments at the uni with people I actually liked. To me, to my way of thinking, after seeing and living through the horrors of a totalitarian regime relying entirely on sheer brutal force, seeing the IRA operatives trying to destroy a democratic regime in the country where modern democracy had been invented and was cherished, was the crime of all crimes. Their activities were nothing short of evil and they were to be exterminated at any cost. I was pretty radical regarding the Irish problem at the time. Merry's husband, a writer, whom I had met a few times, once asked me directly:

"How come an intelligent person like you can have such extreme views?" and he really wanted an answer.

In fairness I must admit that I never even tried to find an answer to this particular question. It was a matter of right or wrong, and the IRA were wrong, simply wrong and I was on the side of 'the right'!

I was in London during much of the IRA bombing campaigns and at times I took the advice of the police and walked avoiding parked cars, a bit hard in South Kensington with cars parked by the students and professors alike all over the place with scant regard for parking rules to start with. The bombing of Harrods and the killing of a woman police constable brought the nasty reality closer to home. Apparently, the IRA would make a phone call telling the British police that a bomb had been planted and the place where the bomb had been planted and how many minutes before it would explode. To me that was an extraordinary way of behaving and one nagging question remained; as part of this 'agreement' with the British security forces, what had the IRA received in return? I was firmly convinced that the British forces behaved in an exemplary manner and defended them at some Islington and Hampstead parties in North London, where I was never invited again, after expressing my honest and obviously correct views about the evil of the IRA! To prove my point the IRA also assassinated people without giving prior notice of any sort: there was the blowing up of a respected member of parliament and of course there was the Brighton bombing, no five minutes warning at that one; that was the nearest the IRA had come to killing Mrs Thatcher and most of her Cabinet and I was extremely relieved when I heard that they had failed.

You were lucky this time, but we only need to be lucky one time, or something on these lines was the rueful statement from the IRA which I really enjoyed reading. They might as well give up, I thought, before realising that this conflict bubbling here and there as Ron would say, had been going on for centuries and without much sign of ending soon.

What really amazed me was the number of Irish people living in London, though not that many in Chelsea. We might have had one or two invited to Merry's parties occasionally. They were not refugees as I wrongly assumed to start with, but economic migrants – legally established dwellers. Apparently, their Irish passport gave them the unimpeded right to live and work in Britain. How extraordinary, I thought, surely this is ridiculous. And to exacerbate my puzzlement, one day when I was in a pub in Maida Vale or nearby, someone called with a collection box for the prisoners of H block, or the IRA mass murderers as I knew then and most papers told me about every single day! I sincerely hoped that someone would mug the IRA sympathiser and his bloody collection box!

Many years later, when some sort of peace treaty was reached with the political wing of IRA and they became part of the political establishment (nobody knows for how long), it turned out that secret discussions had been taking place for many years – even at the peak of the IRA bombing campaigns – while every politician on both sides was swearing blind that nothing could be further from the truth!

The story of the violin

There was bad news even in the ever so cosy and charmed world of Drayton Gardens. Phone rang very early one morning, before seven o'clock, a very rare occurrence indeed and the news was somewhat distressing for Merry. Her favourite aunt had just died and we both then trekked all the way to Twickenham where her Aunt

Ellie (for Elisabeth) had lived a very quiet and I assume pleasant life for most of her years, dedicated mainly to her favourite charity, a sanctuary for donkeys in some remote forest in the south west of the country to which she had given repeatedly large amounts of her inherited money. She had also given to other various charities, to my bafflement and amazement! I met Merry's Aunt Ellie a few times and I always found her much more interesting than her general appearance and demeanour might have suggested. She was always dressed in something velvety in rich colours, mainly deep Bordeaux, very Edwardian I thought. Merry once explained to me that the only thing that Aunt Ellie wore that had some sort of connection with the present day was the watches, big items with some of the largest and clearest displays I'd ever seen. Apparently, the shy, withdrawn and ever so modest Aunt Ellie had had her little bit of vanity and she had been very good at hiding it except for wearing those extravagant and rather big watches. Aunt Ellie had been very scrupulous about time keeping but she had been too vain to wear glasses in public hence the oversized watches. No doubt the glasses would have spoiled her entire attire!

Merry's worries about Aunt Ellie leaving everything to a donkey sanctuary turned out to be just a false alarm. True to her form Aunt Ellie had left what the lawyer described as a "considerable amount of cash", all of it, to her favourite charities, but she had left everything else to Merry, including the house in Twickenham Green and all her possessions. It was my first encounter with a 'changed' Merry, the calm, unemotional, pragmatic businesswoman, and I got a deep feeling of uneasiness, but not for long. The house left by Aunt Ellie was sold within a few weeks to a builder for re-development; all the possessions were brought to Drayton Gardens including a 'lady's violin' in its original 17th century case, about which later.

Neither Merry nor I attended Aunt Ellie's funeral; Merry found it too distressing and time-consuming anyway, and she was right in a certain way. She was very busy going through the papers left by Aunt Ellie, and to my surprise she was horrified at what she found while reading the list of shares left by Aunt Ellie; it turned out that the 'saintly' Aunt Ellie had been a senior shareholder in tobacco companies. "Can you believe it?" shouted a shocked Merry, and in her typical manner took action straight away. She called her stockbroker and asked that all shares in tobacco companies be sold immediately, at "the best possible price", of course. Given the size of the transactions involved, Merry and I got invited by her stockbroker to a tour of the Stock Exchange as his guests. This was in 1983 and the old Stock Exchange was still working with 'old fashioned habits and equipment' – a man's word was his bond and shouting louder than anybody else around was the main equipment! Merry was deeply impressed during our lunch in an exquisite restaurant in the City, while I started having a sort of uneasiness about the whole set-up, Stock Exchange and others! How could people make money, enormous amounts of money, '*lots* of Money' as Mrs Thatcher's mantra would have it, just by shouting the odds? Those traders were making hundreds of times more than the highest paid worker who, in atrocious weather conditions out in the North Sea, was extracting the same precious oil whose price was being savagely speculated … and *for what?* Who benefited most? Definitely not the guys working offshore! Apparently, according to Mrs T, it was the country that benefited – and at that time I took her word for it.

After lunch Merry took the advice of her stockbroker and invested all money from the tobacco companies' shares into a very promising company, British Aerospace, that apparently was bound to get a huge contract from Saudi Arabia with the net result that in the following months Merry's shares had doubled in value – and she had done absolutely nothing except to take her stockbroker's advice. Oh yes, the reason for the jump in the share price was that British Aerospace had got the contract with the Saudis to supply hundreds of planes and God only knows how many other deadly weapons to play with in their desert. Still, Merry was very happy with her investment and I decided to wait for a better time to mention that perhaps the tobacco companies had not been all that bad after all.

In the meantime we were both busy sifting through the myriad of Aunt Ellie's many small possessions deciding what was for keeping, what was to be given to the many charities shops peppered around King's Road and what was simply to be disposed of (an elegant way of saying 'dumped'). However, among the hundreds of little bits and pieces which covered most of the floor in the sitting room, was an item, a puzzling one – Aunt Ellie's old violin. It was no doubt a very old violin, most likely centuries old if its case was anything to go by, and strangely small, more like a child's violin than a standard sized one. Merry would have liked to have kept it but there was no room in the flat despite its two sitting rooms and four bedrooms and just three people living in it (Merry, Ben and I), plus the occasional relative visitor from Merry's large family; still, the place was full of paintings and antiques that wouldn't look out of place in a decent country museum. While considering the various options Merry hit the charity mood and unexpectedly suggested:

"You know that violinist friend of yours, what's his name, Kiri or something like that; you know, the one we gave the old piano to? He might like it, let him have it, ask him to come and we'll give it to him."

Kiri was a Romany violinist that I met while helping the refugee council with translations and the like. As a political refugee he had one of the strangest stories to tell. There he was living quietly in some remote village in *Oversylvania*, playing his violin at funerals, weddings and as required by the people in power and with money. Nothing much happened in his life until he unwittingly became embroiled in some sort of political dispute during a country wedding's celebrations. As a rule of thumb *Oversylvanian* country weddings go through an unbroken ritual that goes something like this:

Sunday afternoon the guests sort of get together, everybody happy to meet everybody else, everybody kisses everybody else and everybody gets dreadfully drunk and then, by about three o'clock in the morning, anybody still standing is either fighting or trying to punch whoever happens to be nearby. Of course, the musicians, 'the bloody gypsies' as they're locally known, are meant to keep on playing, so no fight however fierce will stop the wedding celebrations. There is a line drawn at someone being killed, but that is a rather rare event, about one in every ten weddings or so.

Still, with time, Kiri got a great reputation not only for being an exceptionally talented violinist but also for his calm and placid attitude at even the most raucous weddings and for contributing a great deal at pacifying the warring factions just by playing the violin totally unconcerned for his safety or anybody's else. His violin playing acted as some sort of peacemaker even in the worst situations. So much so that his fame got to the ears of high-ranking comrades and strangely enough it was decided to send Kiri to London of all places to perform during the tricky negotiations between *Oversylvania* and the United Kingdom about the British owned companies which had been seized by the communist regime. If there is anything in any dictatorship that is more bizarre than anything else in any other part of the world, it is the amount of extraordinarily ridiculous decisions. Should there ever be some sort of Olympic competition for the most idiotic decisions taken at the highest level, *Oversylvania* would be on the podium every time!

Of course, Kiri was not to be trusted. The main food for any dictatorship is security paranoia and an inexhaustible reservoir of 'enemies of the people'! Trusting nobody is the first rule of any self-respecting dictator and allowing one's people to travel abroad, and not only any abroad, but the enemy abroad at that is a big no-no – and clearly any dictatorship has more enemies than an *Oversylvanian* sheepdog has fleas! One way or another,

Kiri and his violin and a 'guardian angel' (captain in the *Oversylva-nian* secret services) arrived in London as part of the *Oversylvanian* delegation, and were installed in a very posh but discreet hotel in Roland Gardens where he performed every evening to the exhausted and half inebriated comrades while planning his escape. To fool his guardian angel one day Kiri pretended to go for a walk early in the morning leaving his violin in its case behind, as a clear indication that he would not defect. He never went anyway without his violin, except this time he did. He left the hotel and went hurriedly towards Chelsea police station where he asked for political asylum. Somehow the desk sergeant, most used to dealing with drink driving offences and ritually indulged by the local aristocracy, didn't really know what to do with Kiri and so resorted to the best course of action under the circumstances. As most 'natives' do quite successfully, he passed the problem to someone else and directed Kiri to the Croydon offices of Lunar house, to the Office for Aliens. Kiri, whose English was less than rudimentary, resorted to his small dictionary where he found the word 'alien' but unfortunately it was translated as 'being from a different planet' which deeply confused Kiri. There was no way that he would be going to that place in Croydon, full of 'aliens' from different planets, no doubt. All Kiri wanted was to stay in London and play his violin! He slept for a couple of nights in Kensington Gardens until somebody took him to the British Council, where he was put in touch with a charity dealing with refugees and subsequently put in a hostel for a few weeks – it was the same charity that had helped me a few years earlier and I was happy to oblige with translations and assist him with the first few steps of freedom that most refugees find bewildering at times.

The charity that helped me and many others like me was run by a couple of women I took to be old spinsters, always pleasant, quite charming and who always, but always, found a solution to whatever problem their charity encountered. They even managed somehow to recover Kiri's violin from the *Oversylvanian* delegation! – in the years that have passed, due to the nature of my work, I have encountered many companies and administration set-ups of the highest order but none of them have come anywhere near the efficiency and professionalism of this charity. I still wonder whatever happened to those ever smiling, fragile-looking and welcoming ladies.

Kiri eventually got a very well paid job playing his violin in some of the best hotel restaurants in London and settled in a small flat in the Swiss Cottage area; he also got invited to play at one of Merry's Chelsea parties, where he was greatly appreciated and frankly admired by everybody, including, believe it or not, the musical critic of the Telegraph, a rather morose and distant character, who nonetheless felt obliged to advise Kiri that his harmonies were "not up to scratch" and needed "improving". I was fuming, as Kiri was my discovery and I felt that any less than enthusiastic comment was not to be accepted. However, Kiri assured me that the musical critic was right and that he did need to practise his harmonies, but he required a piano for that, which he could not afford at the time.

Not to worry, Merry intervened. We had a piano, the one in the music room. He could have it; we were reorganising the flat and we never used it anyway, so Kiri was welcome to it! Kiri found two helpers, his next door neighbours, strong guys used to working on building sites who somehow managed to shift the piano to Kiri's flat without doing too much damage. But with improvements came more requirements and Kiri's violin was no longer suitable for the new type of music, popular classics, Kiri had to play for the more sophisticated 'audiences' in The Dorchester and The Ritz.

Merry, who had become very interested in Kiri's progress and his easy adaptation of a new form of music was thoroughly impressed, so much so that through her contacts she got some of the top professors from The Royal College of Music to listen to Kiri's way of playing the violin; as a result Kiri got a 'gig' (funny word this one!) at a charity gala at The Royal Albert Hall, no less.

Of course, Merry and I walked the few hundred yards to The Albert Hall, and all the while I pondered the changes, twists and turns of my life; when I'd been in dear old *Oversylvania* and had dreamt of living in London, just to be there, I would kiss the streets in that miraculous place; please God just let me be there, please God … and a mere three years later, I was furious that when it rained I couldn't get a bloody taxi for love nor money!

"Well," Merry smiled, "that is your nature, you've been born with it and that's the one you'll die with. It is like the colour of your eyes, try as you might it will stay the same!"

Not if you use contact lenses, I almost replied, but I kept it to myself. Let Merry have her little victory for the time being.

At The Royal Albert Hall, when reading the programme we discovered that Kiri had somehow drawn the short straw; he was to perform after a duo of two young sisters, a real musical sensation, extremely popular and almost every other day on radio or TV.

"Oh dear, what an act to follow," Merry sighed. "Let's hope everything goes well for Kiri and his violin."

The girl duo was a real sensation; they got a long, standing ovation and all I thought about was how Kiri would follow that. Eventually, when the ovation for the duo had finished and almost everybody had relaxed exhausted back in their chairs, Kiri's name was announced. No fanfares or strong presentation, just Kiri with his warm smile and dressed in his lucky jacket he had brought from *Oversylvania* and his somewhat dodgy old violin. He started playing his violin and play he did. Over decades, The Royal Albert Hall has been host to many extraordinary violinists but here was a new one for all those privileged to hear Kiri playing. He started modestly by his standards, a Czárdás by Liszt in his own arrangement, extremely fast and furious, followed by something from Mozart's fourth violin concerto and then came the final bit of Kiri's recital. I did not recognise it straight away, but soon it became clear that he was trying and succeeding in playing a concerto for two violins on his almost clapped out single instrument: Kiri was playing Bach's concerto for two violins on one violin, his own, and somehow he managed to create the sound of both violins in one. The skill and dexterity of his playing made the audience gasp and I've never seen so many open mouths and dropped jaws, including Merry's. Kiri's performance was nothing short of extraordinary and when he had finished, he kept the same warm smile and bowed modestly to the most extraordinary ovation. It was very much like the last night of The Proms, but with music only. It took several minutes for the audience to recover and even longer for the calls of "more, more" to subside. Kiri kept his smile unaffected, showing little other emotion and repeating a never-ending thank you, thank you and thank you again.

When we spoke after the show all he expressed was his worries for the state of his violin:

"I was terrified for the strings not to break," he explained in his heavily accented English. "I did not practise much, but I was lucky."

Good grief I told myself, he *was* lucky! Lucky to have that extraordinary talent, that is luck. I was so impressed with Kiri that I made a mental note not to think of him or refer to him in my usual blunt manner 'that bloody gypsy' ever again. Kiri was really good, whatever his origin! Mind you, Merry would always tell me off whenever I called Kiri 'a bloody gypsy' by pointing out that was I then a *'bloody Oversylvanian'*? and she may have had a point; I never found a proper witty reply to her argument and I had better drop it and watch my language!

It was, however, Kiri's evening; he'd already had offers from different agents, which would be dealt with later, tomorrow or after, meanwhile even his violin problem was suddenly solved. Merry would offer him Aunt's Ellie's violin which anyway was just gathering dust in its case somewhere in Merry's workshop – one of the many bedrooms in the flat having been converted in a jewellery workshop for Merry to indulge in her hobby of making unique jewellery items, exotic forms and lots of delicate handiwork!

Kiri gratefully accepted the rather small violin and we didn't hear from him for a few weeks. One day, however, he turned up at the flat un-announced with the violin in its case and explained to both Merry and me in much improved English that he could not use the violin, not properly anyway, and he would like us to have it back and please to not feel hurt.

"You see the neck of the violin is too small for playing vast cadenzas or even faster arrangements," which were his speciality and forte, Kiri explained and anyway he had made enough money to buy a very good second-hand violin that suited 'brilliantly' his style. It was well understood. we wished Kiri the best of luck, as he was embarking on a European tour with a well-known orchestra. He had already asked for and been granted British Citizenship; somehow, he had been fast-tracked for it. So, with a British passport Kiri was gone.

Fancy that, I thought, he's only been here four years and he's already a British citizen with British passport and everything! I almost said 'Bloody Gypsy' but Merry's stare stopped it in its tracks. Then I remembered the old *Oversylvanian* saying that envy is the only vice with no profit or pleasure, so I quickly backtracked to the latest favourite ground, the high moral one!

We still had to deal with Aunt Ellie's old violin and in almost despair I decided to take it and try to 'flog it' (one of Merry's favourite expressions mimicked by myself with my personal touch, a touch of nonchalance, as only a true Frenchman would do!).

I did it in a well thought out plan, after all, I had recently become Project Control Manager of an important oil and gas company, being responsible for project controls within the company; the task of flogging an old violin should be a doddle! (I'm rather proud of my ever increasing and improving vocabulary, but there's still a long way to go towards achieving the two hundred thousand words of the blessed English language!) According to my well planned strategy I would approach the Auction houses first; there was one around the corner in Old Brompton Road in which I strayed now and then on my way from South Kensington station and usually compared their wares to the exquisite, centuries old furniture in Merry's flat. There was no contest, Merry's flat won hands down. The race was much closer as far as paintings were concerned but I still thought Merry's flat won it by a short head! As it happened, my offer of placing the violin was turned down straight away as the violin was no doubt a child's one and they didn't think there was a real market for such a thing. Four Auction houses later I was still carrying my small size violin and even smaller hopes of being able to get rid of it. By then I was contemplating Portobello Market on the following Saturday morning when it would be crowded and full of interested tourists, but at that moment I found myself in Bond Street.

I had just been turned down by the flagship House of Sotheby's, when I noticed a very impressive shop full of musical instruments, top of the range pianos; a most impressive full size Bösendorfer graced the entrance and as a last resort I stepped in.

I was greeted in what I call the 'classic English manner' by an old gentleman with the most reassuring accent. I explained to the helpful gentleman my desire to sell the curious little violin and the old gentleman offered a sympathetic ear. He studied the violin with extreme care, and I hoped he was going to offer me at least fifty pounds (my mental bottom price based on what was my daily income in 1984). But the old gentleman, after a long and thorough examination of the violin said:

"This is interesting, would you please leave this violin with us for a week or two, I'd like to consult with a more knowledgeable specialist than myself, if that is all right with you, Sir." There was only one reply I was in a position to give and almost relieved I settled to see him again in a fortnight.

I almost missed my appointment with the old gentleman in the music shop in Bond Street, nearly forgot it, other more pressing events were taking place in Merry's household and there were some problems with her son's school as well. When I went back to the shop I was firm in my mind on the negotiating position; I would accept nothing less than fifty pounds – as any inexperienced price negotiator will know, I should have considered what would be the *highest* acceptable offer deemed acceptable.

This time the old gentleman asked me to take a seat, enquired if I'd like a cup of tea, which I thought would be very nice (I'd at least get a cup of tea if nothing else for all my efforts with the curious little violin that nobody seemed to want). But the old gentleman had news for me, interesting news, that is.

"We've had a good look at your violin, Sir, and we'd like to make you an offer but first of all could you tell us how you came to have it, Sir?"

I told the old gentleman the full story, Merry's aunt dying and leaving the violin to Merry with the house and innumerable bric-a-brac and the like. The old gentleman listened carefully; he was trying to find out how long the violin had been in the family.

"Well, for all I know it must have been for generations, more than a couple of hundred years if Merry has her dates right, or so I believe to be but I could check on it."

"Yes, I thought so, *we* thought so," repeated the old gentleman, somewhat relieved now that he knew so many details about the violin's provenance. The old gentleman then looked me straight in the eye and with a weak voice said "Would you accept twenty-five, Sir, for your violin?"

Big, big disappointment, just poncey twenty-five pounds and coming all the way to Bond Street; at least I'd had a decent cup of tea and rather tasty biscuit!

As if he'd guessed my thoughts, the old gentleman added candidly:

"I mean, twenty-five *thousand* pounds, in case I did not make myself clear first time."

In 1984 twenty-five thousand pounds was about what I earned a year working on the oil fields of the North Sea (running the (illegal?) betting shop on the oil platform was extra); this amount would also buy a nice, old and solid house in Kemptown, Brighton, that Merry desired so much. I completed the formalities there and then and half an hour later I walked into Drayton Gardens and offered Merry the cheque for twenty-five thousand pounds made out in her name – it was her violin after all.

A trip to Brighton was decided for the very next day, although Merry would have liked to have gone immediately, but frankly, it was a bit late in the day. While Merry was overwhelmed with the unexpected windfall, I was more concerned with the lesson I'd just learned from the old gentleman in the music shop. How could someone who obviously made a good living from buying and selling (people for whom I had no respect or time, having been brought up – as advocated by both the Church and the communist regime (strange union this one!) – to regard them and their wares as a 'necessary evil'), have turned out to be the most honest and correct person I'd ever dealt with? I tried to find an explanation from Merry, but she just brushed away my unease

"He was just *fair* in his dealings with you my dear boy, and that is all. I wouldn't expect an establishment like his to behave in any other way."

This explanation was reinforced by Merry's mother who for reasons of her own added

"Of course, that's what one expects from an establishment which has been around for centuries. Very fair indeed and never taking advantage of someone's ignorance at any time!"

And there was something else, the word 'fair' or rather 'it is not fair' or 'this is fair enough'. As far as I knew then there was no such word in any other language in the world. It didn't mean that other people were fair or not fair but somehow they didn't seem to have a word for it.

* * *

The house at No. 14, Marine Gardens, the oldest building in Kemptown, became Merry's property within a couple of weeks; everything went smoothly, except for a bit of a dispute with the estate agents who took their time removing their big 'For Sale' sign … and that was the last of the Aunt's Ellie's violin story. Not quite. The act of sheer honesty from quarters I had least expected will live with me forever; it was the first time someone dealing with me had treated me fairly. There is no translation for this word 'fair' in *Oversylvania*; this little gesture made me understand and admire these marvellous people I am privileged to live amongst. I have done nothing, really, for this great nation which has offered me sanctuary and treats me with respect and consideration I did not even knew existed. And not for the first time do I feel the deepest gratitude for each single person I see around me.

I promised then in my mind that whatever I was to invent would be first and foremost for this country and its people who gave me asylum.

My feelings of gratitude for fair play were not in the least affected when, a couple of years later, by chance passing Sotheby's in St James's, I noticed an announcement for the sale of an Amati violin, guide price over half a million pounds. I went inside, I looked closely at the violin and there was something familiar about it; at a very close examination I recognised the certain small indentations on the body of the violin. It was, without doubt, Aunt's Ellie's violin, but only part of it. The neck of the violin was different, a bigger and better fit for the rest of the violin's body. I enquired further and eventually the full story emerged. Yes, the violin's body was from an old lady's violin, but only the body; the original neck had at one time been replaced with a small one, most likely to make a violin for a child or a person with very small hands. What the present owners of the violin had managed to do was to track, against all odds, the original neck, and masterly put the violin together. It was being offered at auction and had attracted a great deal of interest and most likely would achieve a new record price for such an instrument. Strangely, the first thought was 'bully for you' for the owner and I was not in the least annoyed that I might have got more money for the violin. They had offered me a fair price which was a thousand time more than I had expected; my dealing with them had been fair and above board; after all, they must have put a great deal of effort and money into this enterprise and now they would get their reward. Well done, I thought, and I still think that today, although the violin sold for twice the expected price, to an undisclosed bidder whom I would dearly have liked to have met to tell him the true story of the violin.

I couldn't resist, however, telling Kiri the story when I met him on a flight to Abu Dhabi. There he was in the business class next to a furious sheikh from Abu Dhabi who by some clerical error on the part of the airline had been placed in business class instead of the first class he'd actually paid for. He was from the local ruling family and also Kiri's employer; a very, *very* angry gentleman – and if that was anything to go by not the type you'd wish as your employer unless really desperate.

I told Kiri the full story including the final price the violin was sold for. The net result was that Kiri finished the duty free bottle of Cognac I had reserved for myself. I came to the conclusion that telling people interesting stories about a strangely shaped violin was not always beneficial to the teller!

There is a postscript to this little story. The Abu Dhabi sheikh had overheard the story and thought it was extraordinarily funny and invited me to see him in Abu Dhabi – he must have been someone important because at the airport he just whisked me through the passport and customs control for which I was very grateful. I met the gentleman again as my curiosity was aroused, not having met an Abu Dhabi 'native' before. I was also curious as to why on earth he should be wearing several wrist watches, one more expensive that the other but only one of them was showing the correct real time (of course it had to be the most expensive of them all). When I asked him eventually why he did that, he looked puzzled and replied curtly

"Because only the most expensive one must show the right time, the rest follow behind according to their value!"

And there was one more astonishing surprise to come. The local sheikh was the new owner of what had once been Aunt Ellie's old violin; the proud owner of an extremely rare violin on which Kiri could no longer practice, just perform, and not for everybody, but for a selected few – selected personally by the sheikh that is! Good luck Kiri!

Charity and loneliness

If somebody would bother to make a top ten list of what is the word most used in Chelsea, I predict that 'charity' would be at the very top at all times. There was almost always a hush of reverence whenever the word charity was pronounced by Merry's mother; pronounced possibly is not the right word, *annunciated*, perhaps would be more appropriate. As a first hand beneficiary of a great deal of charity from people I had never seen before, people who not only spent money in helping me, but most likely spent time and energy as well, which impressed me even more; after all anyone very rich can give you a few pennies, but for someone grand and important to take an interest in my wellbeing, well, that was something new and extraordinary. Especially as no one here had ever used the word altruism, which I think most people around have shown plenty of but would never accept as such.

I could see Merry's mother rejecting any idea that she 'suffered' from altruism ("whatever that is!") in a style not dissimilar to an Opera Diva's final scene. Partly to amuse myself, I would provoke her to some sort of conversation about her favourite charities with the net result that I was always put in my place ... to start with. There was as usual a bit of wickedness (see, I can use long words!) in me, just to amuse myself at times

"One does not discuss one's favourite charities, as you well know" was her terse response. I bet she meant to include "with the likes of you" but to preserve the family harmony most likely she stopped just short of it! She was much too grand to go into 'boring, little details'.

Apparently, Britain is the world capital of charity work, there are many thousands if not tens of thousands of dedicated, professionally run charities, officially recognised, helping the most diverse and some would say curious causes and aims, and that is 'curious' by British standards, which says a lot!

There was one particular charity that Merry would mention quite often, the one in some forest far away in the west of the country concerned with the welfare of donkeys and in which her rather well to do Aunt Ellie had taken a keen interest and who had been giving a great deal of money for donkey's years! Merry's main worry, which she never admitted openly, was that Aunt Ellie would leave all her 'substantial' estate – that is substantial according to a Mr Isaacs, QC, one of Merry's long-time and deeply respected friends, and the family lawyer. Once I asked Merry why on earth she needed a lawyer all the time and the answer was rather puzzling:

"My dear boy, this country, this great country, the one we all call Great Britain is a country made by the lawyers for the benefit of the lawyers, and that is the way things are!"

Bang goes another preconception I had about Britain – I thought it was all done by the inventiveness and diligence of those superior beings who invented almost everything that was worth inventing – now I was being told by a most reliable source that it was all due to people dreaming up laws, applying those laws and milking the profits in the process!

"Some call it *democracy*, my dear boy," a smiling Mr Isaacs explained slowly and firmly. "Please, don't take my word for it, just look at the facts. In the British parliament, mother of all democracies, old or newcomers, there are six hundred and fifty members, out of which more than seventy per cent are lawyers by training – I rest my case!" And Mr Isaacs, QC, with a highly respected Chambers in the City, was not joking. As time passed his assertion turned out to be more truthful than ever. Still, to my mind I still thought that democracy was there where the minority had the right to tell the majority 'you are wrong' and 'why don't you do something about it?'. However, having the power to implement this dictum seems to be the main problem yet to be sorted out!

After my extremely successful forays in the oil exploration in the North Sea, I was financially almost secure, and all through sheer hard work, no cheating, no financial dodgy trades, not even fooling anyone, except perhaps myself – but only at chosen times and occasions! There I was cruising in King's Road in my Lotus Esprit (limited black edition of only forty cars!) with full speed of five miles per hour behind a smelly, black smoke spewing bus, or even worse, behind a taxi deliberately blocking the road feeling proud and extremely happy with myself. Of course, I realised that my showing off was there just to satisfy my ever-growing vanity and a bit of 'slow down Michael' was bound to come, as usual, from an unexpected source. Ben was doing quite well at his 'posh' school in Westminster, was growing into being a very thoughtful young boy and while applauding my 'successes' there was a note of caution in his congratulations – a note of pragmatism in his attitude. To me it was amazing to hear a thirteen-year-old child capable of such mature thinking, at times much more than mine.

"OK," said Ben, "now you've got yourself an expensive car, the latest sports car most people can only dream of, the most desirable hi-fi system and you spend a fortune on clothes and entertaining. And to top it all you and mother have bought yourselves one of the oldest houses in Brighton, not bad for eight years, not bad at all…" But he was not finished. "So, what is the next trick? What are you going to do next?" he insisted sternly, with all the seriousness of a thirteen-year-old.

I had to reply, and I heard myself saying:

"I will do a great deal of charity work, starting today if you want to know."

"Oh yes," Ben dismissed my offer. "Can you tell me which charity would that be? I *know you* Michael," – he stressed the words 'know you' – "all you'll do is sign a cheque to make you feel good and that is that! I *know* you."

What on earth do they teach him in that bloody school, I wondered. What sort of attitude was that anyway? I promptly thought of a proper line of reasoning to silence this acerbic and ironic critic.

"I shall go and do voluntary work for *Help the Aged*, you'll see."

"Good," said Ben and two hours later he turned up with a list of telephone numbers all belonging to various charities for helping the aged all over London. I chose one at random and Ben looked satisfied and congratulated me

"Well done, you've chosen one in the East End, in a very poor area. Good luck to you, you'll need it, but not as much as the poor old people in that area."

I promptly contacted the local charity and they were absolutely delighted to have a volunteer with time to spare. It turned out that all they required was a person with a car and time to take old people to the big supermarkets miles away where there were plenty of bargains and offers that the old people with not much mobility would find very useful.

"Great," said Merry, when I mentioned my next 'venture', "but we must find you a white van for your new venture! You can't possibly go there in a Lotus Esprit, unless you want to lose your wheels, you know that area has a bit of a reputation and a second or even third hand white van, whitish at least, is the appropriate vehicle and in keeping with the local surroundings! You'll have to mix in and better dress yourself in a track suit, not a new one though!"

As it happened, at the end of the 1980s, track suits were all the rage as far as new fashion went! Even Chanel joined the craze, or should I say *created* the craze to start with. Luckily for me, just by chance I had already discovered English fashion. (Oh yes, it does exist and it is the best in the world – don't take my word for it though, just take a little walk down Jermyn Street, not to mention Savile Row, and you'll see what a gentleman's attire ought to look like, that is if you have the taste or inclination for the finer, more sophisticated things in life; something you must be born with, or, in special cases like me, have the taste and intelligence for!) But more about my sartorially adventurous taste in a future chapter – I am writing about my help for poor aged people in this one!

Before my first venture into deepest East End of London, I put my Esprit in a garage after carefully sticking a notice in the back window stating for everyone to see MY OTHER CAR IS A WHITE VAN which I thought was very witty, but Ben was unimpressed. He and a mate of his from the scouts, both showed their displeasure the only way teenagers are so good at – by ignoring me!

Feeling uplifted and full of creative enthusiasm I made it to the address in Catford, where a small charity helping the aged with no means of transport available was based. I was greeted by the usual pleasant, middle-aged lady (who seemed to be the stereotype for most charity workers I had met thus far), all warmth and happiness. Obviously, she was more than delighted to see me and introduced herself with barely restrained enthusiasm. I sincerely wondered how on earth every British person working for charity could be so full of goodness and enthusiastic hope, and Carmen (her name) was no exception.

"Frankly, I was not sure that you would turn up. It is so kind of you to spare the time and effort, we are really so grateful," she enthused. I felt slightly embarrassed and Carmen was only happy to explain.

"If you wonder about my name, Carmen, that is because my father was Spanish. Small world as you can see." I smiled politely and ventured some sort of reply:

"Well, I have the time and opportunity and, you see, I'd like to help, if I may."

"Of course, you may, as much as you want. But first I'll have to show you the ropes, as it is. You will be helping elderly people with their shopping. Just drive them to the supermarket of their choice, carry their shopping back to the car, and then take their shopping to their flat, help them to unpack if they don't mind, especially the heavy stuff, and that's all. You do have a car with you?"

"Yes, I've got a white van," I replied and seeing her puzzled expression I elaborated further:

"I was led to understand that there would be three or four people to help, so I thought a van would be most appropriate, lots of room and easy parking." (Well, I hadn't really meant parking, I thought something on the lines of safety, but I let it pass!) But Carmen understood:

"Oh, I see, well, I'd better explain. You'll find that older people protect their independence at all costs. There are people who'd rather go hungry than be part of a shopping group. For them shopping is private, one of the very few private activities left to them; you'll have to take everyone separately when you go shopping and it would be better not to mention the others. What we are doing is helping them, making their lives a bit more comfortable, not intruding on their independence. OK?" Carmen looked me straight in the eye searching perhaps for my understanding and perhaps approval – or assessing me to see if I was the right person for that particular charity.

"The first person we are going to see is Angela, she prefers to be called Angie, and she is a sweetie."

Later I learned that as far as Carmen was concerned, everyone her little charity dealt with was "a sweetie" and I made a mental note to place the word 'sweetie' at the top of my vocabulary.

As it happened, Angela, "please call me Angie", had lost her husband seven years previously and was finding living on her own and taking care of herself a real struggle. Of course she promptly offered the traditional cup of tea but Carmen insisted that we go straight away to the nearest supermarket and get on with it, there were three other people waiting their turn, and Carmen was sure that Angie would show me the ropes while shopping – nothing could be easier. She also passed me the details of the other people to help shopping after I'd finished with my first client, Angie.

I helped Angie to the van and helped her slim frame to climb onto the passenger's seat, thinking that I should get a normal car next time, and we hit a snag straight away. I enquired about directions:

"Which supermarket shall we go to Angie, which one would you prefer?" But Angie wasn't listening; she was busy telling me things about her life and many other things – perhaps we should have had the cup of tea first and let her talk at her leisure before going. Of course, she had no one to talk to all day long; I don't think she even had a cat, just an old TV in the corner of her poorly furnished bedsit.

"I am eighty-one, you know," she informed me with the pride of a long-distance runner. "Is this your van, or you've just nicked it? I don't want to be arrested, you know," Angie mused worryingly.

"Angie, my dear lady, you must tell me which way to go, where would you like to go?"

But Angie had other things on her mind just at that time, and for a while longer she continued her interrogation.

"Do you know how to drive?"

"Well, I've been doing it for half an hour now, haven't we?"

"Is that all?" She almost jumped, totally misunderstanding my reply.

"Do you have a driving permit?" she enquired, meaning obviously a driving licence, but I let it pass. I stopped the van rather abruptly to the enormous displeasure of a huge lorry driver who made his feelings known by gesticulating wildly and aggressively and then to my amazement and disbelief, the lovely little lady, this respectful older member of society, took the challenge of the lorry driver by gesticulating even more rude gestures accompanied by a colourful vocabulary totally appropriate under the circumstances. Deeply satisfied with her version of 'putting the world to rights' Angie decided to deal with the more mundane aspects of human life and made a good start by at last considering my question about which supermarket would satisfy her particular needs best.

"Shall we go to Asda?" I ventured a small suggestion.

"Oh no, I don't like it there," Angie flatly refused.

"OK, let's try Sainsbury's, they have everything there," was my next prompting, which met an even firmer reply.

"Oh no, they are beastly there, I don't want it," Angie replied with the determination of a three-year-old.

Not to worry, as chance would have it, we were just passing the local Co-op and I pointed it out to Angie who didn't even bother to grace me with a reply. Her look spoke for her and everybody else!

I was running out of options and unless I found something soon, I was going to have to cancel the next 'appointment', which was nothing short of a disaster on my first day of charity work!

Help came from an unexpected corner; it came from Angie herself.

"Somebody told me there is a new store, a cash and carry newly open, not far from my place; can you go there, please?" she enquired sweetly.

"Of course, anywhere, just direct me."

"It is just around the corner from me, I told you once," said Angie, falling back on her first line of defence. She was right, the new 'cash and carry' was open twenty-four hours a day, handy to know and it was within walking distance from Angie's place. She found it to be a very pleasant and friendly shop, and cheaper than all the other ones "who skin you alive". I was so delighted that this particular trip was almost over that I offered to pay for Angie's groceries, despite the advice I got from Carmen against gestures of this nature. Angie refused it anyway, much too proud. She was happy with her groceries and ordering me around.

"Just don't drop them, they cost money, you know. You should know that, even foreigners know that," she concluded with a wide, satisfied smile.

"See you next week, Angie," I shouted from the door.

"See you," she replied. "Don't forget, same time same place!"

I was over an hour late for the next 'appointment' in the area and I was relieved to see that the gentleman I met was pleasant and understanding for the cause of my delay. Gerald, that was his name, looked twenty years younger than his real eighty-two that I almost asked to see his father.

"I knew you'd be late," he said, "taking Angie shopping always takes a long time, she's very fussy, isn't she?" he suggested.

Of course, I could not discuss with anybody my 'charity cases' and I didn't really have to explain to Gerald the complexity of re-lations between helper and the person to be helped. Gerald knew all this pretty well; it just amused him to ask:

"Did you go to all the supermarkets with Angie?"

"Look, I cannot really discuss it, you know it is private."

"Yes, of course," Gerald agreed. "Shame she didn't tell you why she is avoiding all the big supermarkets. I'll tell you anyway," Gerald volunteered while I drove to the rather upmarket Waitrose, his personal choice, because "they are pricy, but their food is very good. Less but best," he repeated, like a commercial jingle and very proud of it, too!

"You should put Angie last on your list; she is a time waster if she feels like it. And, just to let you know, like it or not, the reason she cannot go to any of the big supermarkets is that she has been banned from all of them, every single one." Noticing my puzzled look, he raised the stakes. "Don't ask why, ask her. You'll have a good laugh."

"Look, I just don't want to know, I will not discuss other people with you or anybody else and that is that."

"Please yourself, but you'll have a good laugh when you find out why the frail, gentle and kind lady has been banned from most places."

"Look Gerald, I am not here to amuse myself so please put a stop to it." And then on impulse I added, "We all might have things to hide, things we are not proud of, you know, skeleton in the cupboard and the like."

To my amazement and almost disbelief Gerald shut down completely and gave me a suspicious look.

Months later, when I saw Carmen, Angie, Gerald and the others for the last time before going abroad on a two-year project, Carmen volunteered to share a few of their secrets. It turned out that Angie, the sweetest old lady you could ever imagine, was in fact an inveterate shop-lifter; most stores had got annoyed with her shop-lifting and having to call the police to arrest an eighty-one-year-old woman, yet again, take her to Court and have her fined a sum of money she could not possibly afford to pay, and the authorities would never collect, and so resorted to banning her from entering the store. Having known her quite closely I am certain that her shop-lifting was more her cry for some sort of companionship in her years of blinding loneliness than actual necessity; at times she managed to deal with her loneliness and excused her shop-lifting by stating firmly and with deep belief:

The poor steal for need
The rich steal for greed

But what I noticed and found extraordinary was how much in common there was between the old, lonely, poor woman from the East End and the old, lonely and very rich woman in Chelsea. I looked at Angie and Camilla (Merry's mother) and the closer I looked the more they had in common. Except for accent and their material and social status, there was no difference between Angie, old lady in her tidy, spotlessly clean, smaller than a shoe box council flat (I am not a big person but I found the place had hardly room enough for two people) and Camilla in her five bedroom flat overlooking Hyde Park, full of precious paintings and antiques. They were both lonely in their old age and loneliness does dreadful things to people; it is at its worst for the older lot, of course. Despite popular belief, money protects little and makes things even worse. In the weird way the world works, Camilla had more worries about money than Angie would ever have. Camilla worried non-stop about having her money stolen or miss-appropriated to such a degree that she used to call her bank several times a day, fretted non-stop about her will and frankly I hadn't seen her smile even once in ten years or so. On the other hand, Angie worried about money once a week when collecting her pension from the post office and was worried about being mugged on her way back to her bedsit where she felt safe and content.

They both came from different directions but they met, without knowing or admitting, on the Boulevard of Loneliness, with room for everyone. A much more crowded place every time I look at it, just reinforcing the knowledge that there is a great deal of loneliness in the most crowded places. And still they were both graciously content with their life, suffering in silence whatever fate or whoever might throw at them; all done in silent dignity under the unwritten golden slogan *'one shouldn't make a fuss'*.

I've seen quite a bit in my life and I try to make sense of everything, good or bad, pleasant or deplorable, but I still can't work out where these women found the strength, the power and the inner warmth to face the daily grind and inevitable ending with stoic resignation and ever diminishing physical powers. God only knows how much pain is hidden behind the simple statement, *'one shouldn't make a fuss'* and I hope I will be able to face life with similar fortitude.

I went to see Angie for the last time before going to work on a very lucrative contract in France, and I knew she was in worse health and perhaps she wouldn't make it to her eighty-second Birthday. She had never accepted any presents from me before but this time I managed to convince her that a birthday present would be appropriate.

"What would you like, Angie, for your birthday, something to make you happy and to be useful as well?"

As if expecting my proposal Angie was prepared.

"I tell you what I want, something that I also need. Can I have an iron please?" Then she added an explanation as a sort of excuse for her request. "I want to iron my best dress before… " and then she stopped. I understood the meaning of before and I almost cried in despair.

"OK, your best dress!" Her best dress, according to her own admission, but she only had two dresses, but I skipped this little detail and asked her:

"What type of iron would like?" meaning that there are so many different types of irons, with steam, over steam, more steam, self-regulating, you name it we have it, sort of availability. Angie opened large her kind eyes, an illuminating smile crossed her face and she added casually:

"An electrical one, please!"

Her death upset me greatly for no apparent reason. Still, there is the knowledge that Angie remained Angie to the very end. Even now, it is reassuring for me to think of Angie and her life as the best way to chase away any thoughts of depression or defeat. It works every time. Great present; thank you, Angie!

Integrating – induction and repercussions

As a result of my work in the North Sea, I managed to balance my financial situation greatly in my favour and consequently, when considering which work contract to commit to, I had turned down three serious and very well paid contracts in one week – to Merry's amazement and her mother's half-compliment, "Well, you must be good at something," she croaked. I almost burst with a comment on the lines of "I please your daughter a great deal almost every night, I'm good at other things too!" but managed to control myself – an English gentleman never talks about private matters (well, that is something I read somewhere!)

I joined Amnesty International. Mark, Merry's cousin, 'reassured' me that MI5 kept a list of all Amnesty International members, I assumed for their own protection, but I might have been wrong on that one! I also gave a nice sum as a donation to the same organisation but I had that itch – the one that told me that I could do more and better, if I just thought about it.

How do you really help a refugee? What would make his life easier and meaningful? What would help him or her most of all? Integration. This is the main ingredient in every refugee's life. Integration makes the most meaningful change; it transforms his or her blind, exhausting, never-ending toil into meaningful study and work – I strongly believe in it, I can quote myself as an example, modest as I am!

Great, INTEGRATE, that is all nice and good, it is a Power Point sort of slogan (the guy who invented Power Point needs public flogging! Just joking!), the type politicians will take and run with for the rest of their lives. How do you go about actually implementing it? Which are the concrete movements and actions, and the most important? Who is doing what for this process of integration to actually work in an efficient and beneficial way to both the refugees and the 'natives'? It sounds like a very tough nut to crack. (See, I'm making progress all the time, myself!) Suddenly I know what is to be done and, more importantly, *how* it is to be done, in practical terms with all the activities defined, costed and finally implemented, not much different from a project of building a platform in the North Sea! The word is INDUCTION – a standard operation, a well-established sequence of events and actions through which any newcomer is introduced into the ways of the new country and customs and habits of its 'natives'.

* * *

Straight away, I started developing a sort of Induction manual on how to behave and generally how to make your life and the lives of those around more tolerable, even pleasant (and why not?), when you are in a new and unfamiliar place. I learned it from, believe it or not, the oil and gas companies: how to help someone new to integrate in a new team or organisation in the most efficient and trouble-free way. Yes, the same companies accused of irresponsible behaviour as far as the environment is concerned; the same companies who now and then are in and out of courts of law for little 'misdemeanours' like 'marinating in oil' the Gulf of Mexico, polluting beaches and destroying fish reserves; yes, the very same companies contribute a great deal to develop new, more intelligent ways of getting the best from their employees. If they do it out of the goodness of their heart or for some other reasons is debatable, but the results are quite impressive.

The Oil Companies were the first to develop and perfect this system, euphemistically called **induction**, which may look like a waste of time and money at first: a new employee is usually a big cost to the company and to have to spend up to four days being shown the ropes and general company behaviour and expectations involves a great deal of working time for different people of different trades, all with one aim: to create from the start a professional relationship that will pay a good return in the long run, although it costs a fair amount. Well, this induction, if done properly, is extremely efficient in the long run and brings real benefits to all concerned. It makes one feel accepted and almost integrated before doing a scintilla of 'actual' work. Induction looks from the balance sheet point of view a sheer waste of time and money, but if abandoned would be false economy and must be resisted at all costs! This appears a contradiction in terms, but you try and tell that to a finance director and see how far you get!

So, completely hooked on the benefits and advantages of Induction in its most efficient form, I developed pretty fast something that I called **Induction for Refugees**. I printed a small brochure trying to set out in practical terms, things, living essentials, small things, normal things to anyone living in Britain for a while, things taken for granted by most 'natives' but a mixture of dangerous unknowns and pitfalls at every step for refugees, especially contacts with authorities; nothing seems to scare refugees more than any contact with any sort of civil servant – quite a few of them will be worn out and dirty from the long trips they have taken, many will have a small amount of money, carefully put aside and ready to be passed as a bribe to the clerk at the job centre or housing, as they have had to do all their lives before. One of my most difficult tasks is to insist, at times even threaten some refugees not to try and pay a bribe – the threat to send them back if they try it, is the most efficient one. Something often remarked on by many English friends is that very few, if any, refugees ever say 'I'm sorry' or 'excuse me', although sometimes they should – but there is a simple and painful explanation. If they've done something wrong, they are as a rule sorry for what they've done but coming from a climate of terror and fear any admission to other people that they've done something wrong towards the authorities could mean big troubles or could even be fatal.

Based on my own experiences I split the brochure-cum-folder into main relevant sections like:

DEALING WITH AUTHORITIES

with helpful subsections:

Job Centre
Council Housing
Legal Advice
ADMIN section including
GP services (always very helpful)
Banking facilities (this one is perhaps the most difficult of all. I've never been able to properly explain to bona fide political refugees why they might well be denied banking facilities by the same banks who happily provide money-laundering facilities to the rulers and oligarchs who robbed the place blind to start with.)

Wise shopping terribly important, money being extremely scarce. (I've met hundreds of political refugees, all extremely poor by any standards, and even the lucky few, who through their activities have become reasonably well off, mainly by writing books, are incredibly careful with their meagre allowances.)

My main problem, I thought, was the amount of suspicion I encountered from some refugees, but eventually I understood why they were wary of me. In their view, I was somehow associated with the authorities in one form or another, after all I 'knew the ropes' as the saying goes. Even more implicitly suspicious for them was the fact that I never asked for any bribes of any sort, which they found extraordinary.

Work finding work legally is a big problem.

In their wisdom the Home Office at the time had decided that £4 a day was enough subsistence for the political refugees, and officially they were not meant to supplement this meagre income by working, even if they took jobs nobody else wanted, mainly heavy manual work for little money, way below minimum wage.

There are several places in London where a person without all credentials 'available' can find a place of work on a daily or hourly basis just by turning up and being chosen by a sort of 'gang master' or another individual needing unskilled labourers. It doesn't matter how qualified the person looking for work is, the work he is required to do is strictly manual, hard and poorly paid. Places like this are much maligned. They serve people that no official channel does, and it is in the last instance the last help before they starve or resort to begging. Most political refugees are incredibly proud people, pride being one of the few characteristics that survives and keeps them fighting for their ideals. There are frequent examples of former street cleaners, night watchmen etc, who have become the President of their own country, elected in democratic elections, which I always give a cheer for!

But before they can get a legal job, most of them will end up working in the 'black economy' – a silly name but that's what people call it. Almost every day at seven in the morning some of the would-be labourers will be hired, and others not. On one occasion I went with some refugees to understand why some of them would be hired while others not. And I was stupefied to realise that the 'hiring system' worked on the basis of first impressions. The refugee who looked straight in the eye of the would-be 'employer' and smiled openly was hired, while those with the same attributes but who looked morose or unhappy were not. I asked one of the more active 'employers' how he chose who to hire and who not. After some reticence he agreed to tell me:

"Well, I don't know these people from Adam, and if he looks like me or you, looks me in the eye, that's the test. If he can speak some English even better, not much, just to understand what he has to do is enough. I pay him in cash at the end of the day and that's all there is to it and it never fails."

It goes without saying that 'smile and get work' became an essential part of my induction on how to integrate in Britain – with a very good rate of success!

Things went much better than expected to start with. I tried to do my induction for the newly arrived in a professional manner; to each of them I gave my little folder with its various sections.

I contacted one of the boroughs in the East End of London, with a serious influx of immigrants, much more than any other borough in London. There appears to be no equitable sharing of newcomers among the London boroughs, all thirty-three of them. Somehow, the poorer the borough the bigger quota of refugees! Every single government in the last fifty years or so has passed the buck, promised the moon and ended up with a refugee crisis! Still, this particular council showed a great deal of understanding, seemed seriously happy about any help from almost anybody and the net result was that I was allowed to use an office within the council premises to help with my induction. Obviously, I had to pay myself for all the expenses incurred, and that was that.

I convinced six people to come and listen to me in the first session. I was professionally prepared by any standards. I had rehearsed my opening speech with Merry (she seemed sincerely proud of my 'new venture') and off I went!

I remembered to open the proceedings with the biggest smile I was capable of and started as planned in a semi-joking manner. After mentioning the weather, a neutral subject I thought, but they disliked it intensely, I moved quickly on to a more serious subject. Everybody listened intently while I explained in the way I understood what it was like to be a refugee and how to cope and hopefully progress under the circumstances:

"Being an integrated refugee is like a sort of marriage based on tolerance and understanding on both parts," I explained. Later, as a concession to the background of some of the refugees, I changed the word 'marriage' to 'bonding'. "By accepting you the

British authorities will be responsible for giving you initial support and help, will provide you with some sort of survival income and a roof over your head, will treat you for free for whatever health requirements you have, all for free, both by the state and also a myriad of charity organisations run by the most altruistic people you can imagine. All you have to do is to show the same attitude, to answer in kind to kindness, show understanding where you do not understand exactly what is going on and please bear in mind that it was your choice to come to this island nation in the first place. 'Natives' of islands all over the world seem to have this characteristic of being distant and reserved, so they are, this is the nature of this place and its inhabitants. They also like you to say, as they do, 'thank you' and 'please' all the time, it costs nothing but creates a sort of connection that will grow stronger and stronger and believe it or not will make your life a great deal better. They seem to be distant and aloof but that is till they know you better, it may take some time, you must be patient. I applied to join one of the most exclusive Gentleman's Clubs as a student prank, and guess what – twenty-seven years later I got a letter granting me temporary membership from the highly regarded club. You see, all it takes is a bit of time – after all you must not rush things! In this 'bonding of convenience' remember that having to eat soggy chips and drink warm beer is small concession compared to the advantage of safety and full human rights, *real* human rights are taken extremely seriously in this country – after all they have invented most of them, and now they have stick for applying them, come what may." And finally, I did a small calculation, showing them how much the British authorities spent or have allocated to spend (rarely the same thing!) on each refugee coming to Britain. It turned out that on average the cost for each of them was just under the average income of a local working person, which is well above the official poverty line. This had a sobering effect and balanced the equation of supporting the 'influx of refugees' and who would be paying for it – in fairness nothing pleased a refugee more than getting a well-paid job and promptly start moaning about having to pay taxes – becoming British is not as hard as it first looks!

* * *

I also try to explain to them the 'strange' behaviour of the 'natives' at times, reminding them that it is their duty as guests to try and integrate with the local people. I always give myself as an example, a sort of shiny one as it happens. I have had a high rate of success as far as integration is concerned, about eighty per cent (my bar for success was set at seventy-five per cent) so I am quite happy and satisfied with myself in the main and, if truth be told, also with the refugees. Some of them have become real success stories by any meaning of the word.

Past shadows

As a child in *Oversylvania* I was given a map of the world, a bit of a rarity, it was a map of the world without borders, before the Russian occupation and the imposed communist regime. There were so many things to see, so many things to wonder about on that map of the world, beautiful colours, mountain ranges and my mind floated happily on the map of Europe, travelling in all directions. There was much to see and even more to dream about. And then I found something extraordinary on that map. Identifying countries and places I stumbled on a couple of islands with the inscription Great Britain above and London marked as capital. At first, I refused to believe what I was seeing. What, that small, elongated island was the mighty England, no less? It was smaller in size even than *Oversylvania*, it just did not add up, it made no sense. First I thought the map was one of the communist regime's standard bit of disinformation; just show the enemies (Anglo-American was at the time the deadly enemy of the workers' paradise!) and just by showing them as small and puny, brought the day that little bit closer when all-conquering communism would finish them off! Still, for me, as a nine-year-old, there were questions to be asked, answers to be worked out and nobody around to ask. Asking the wrong person even an innocent question could have repercussions under any dictatorship, and a very dreadful one under a strict communist regime. At that time my father was already under arrest and so was my mother, and my elder brother had been sent to a forced labour camp, so practically I had no one to ask this question that kept me awake at night. Eventually, I gathered all my courage and asked the teacher responsible for my class, a kind, extremely fat and always encouraging teacher:

"How could such a small place become such a powerful country, such a fearful force?" I said pointing to Great Britain on the map. "Is this right, just a small place and such a big empire, how can that be?" I insisted with all the naïvety of a nine-year-old that was growing old pretty fast. Mrs Riza, that was the teacher's name, sent me to the corner of class in a stern manner, as a punishment for asking such a stupid thing and I was punished with detention for my pains. I thought that was extraordinarily unfair, as I was by far the best in the class, if not in the school, much more advanced in knowledge and thinking than my fellow pupils. But Mrs Riza came to see me in my detention class and sat next to me and explained in a language I understood what made England, as everybody called it, what it is – at least according to Mrs Riza:

"They, the British, have invented more than anybody else in the world and they have used their inventions and innovations to conquer the world. It is in their character to invent and innovate at all times and that has brought them rewards." Mrs Riza then told me her version of inventing the chronometer and its phenomenal influence in building the British Empire, facts hardly known by anyone else apparently. A British king a few hundred years ago had offered a great deal of money to anyone who could produce a very precise clock, precise to the second, and after many years of work and a great deal of strife, a certain gentleman, Mrs Riza couldn't remember his name, produced just that, a chronometer, made of wooden parts, but a working instrument. Why was it so important that the king paid him in barrels full with gold coins, lots and lots of money, hard to say precisely how much? Because this little wood contraption had made the British Fleet the most powerful fleet in the world almost overnight. They had an advantage nobody else had, they knew almost at all times where they were in the seas and oceans of the world, the Longitude had arrived, and while all the other fleets in the world were just wondering around almost blind, the British Fleet was always compact and had much more manoeuvrability. "And that is how they became so great," concluded Mrs Riza, "because they always invented something to keep them ahead. Now take your books and go home, don't tell anyone what I told you."

That explanation had a huge impact on me and my way of thinking, much more than any lecture I've ever had from anybody and it's stood me best in life. I owe something else to Mrs Riza, a lesson on how to 'manage' under dictatorship and danger and still do the right thing. At the end of the first four years of school, prizes were given to the best pupil. I was unashamedly the best in the school and very proud of it. The day before the prize-giving ceremony, I was told that the school could not be seen to award first prize to the son of a political prisoner and there would be no prizes awarded in that particular year to anybody – that was the best Mrs Riza could do and I am grateful to her to this day. To her and the story of Longitude!

A few years later while in high school, I got my first radio with, what joy, short waves so I could listen at night to all those forbidden sweets: news from the other side! There were radio stations broadcasting from the West to the part of Europe still under communist dictatorship but I was more interested in learning English and someone told me that the best way to learn a foreign language was to listen to radio broadcasts in that language to become familiar with the particular tone and sonority of it. I would find a great deal of satisfaction in listening to the BBC World Service, hardly understanding a word of it, but the tone, the sound was so beautiful to listen to and slowly, slowly I started identifying words.

"This is the BBC World Service" was the sweetest and most melodic 'tune' in that time of my life, especially a certain lady who had a very deep, melodic voice, like a mezzo-soprano, and I'd always understand one extra word when she read the news. (When I later mentioned this detail to Merry, she got very enthusiastic and said we must have a party and invite her, but I found the proposal too intrusive and I didn't want to spoil the past in any shape or form.) For my fellow pupils there was the Beatles music and the like at the time but I preferred the BBC World Service. Of course, I still listen to the BBC World Service but now I understand everything they say, and at times I am not exactly happy! A correction here and there wouldn't go amiss, just to put them right!

With or without first prize I was admitted without any problem to the best school in town, a very old and reputable school where I had a phenomenally good old tutor who encouraged me in my way of thinking and doing things, not an easy or very wise thing to do for someone like me, the son of an *enemy of the people*, sharing the same class room with the son of the chief of the local police. It was me winning prizes for the school in school competitions both in science and sport, so nobody mentioned my parents or my father's fate. That kept me safe and I could indulge in reading the likes of Balzac, Shakespeare, Goethe, all not on the recommended list approved by the communist system. It was a privilege that gave me an unbeatable advantage against the scions of the local dignitaries. It opened my 'intellectual eyes', if you want, at a very early age and prepared me for life to come better than anything else. Mrs Riza my former teacher arranged for me to be taught French by one of her retired friends and twice a week I had lessons in the language of Molière and my all-time favourite, Guy de Maupassant – to my mind obligatory reading for any smart teenager who wants to know about the intimate relations between ladies and gentlemen in a sophisticated, polite manner.

I learned a great deal more, I was given access to the School's Old Library, that was the library that was meant to have been destroyed after the communist takeover but somehow escaped through oversight, or laziness, or sheer spite against the communist regime. This library survived almost intact and most importantly I could read to my heart's pleasure and fascination, books published 'before' (meaning before the Russian invasion with all its dire consequences, to last for generations), and consequently have in my mind a more balanced view of the world having found some truths about the United Kingdom, eventually finding the answer to one question that had long bothered me: how come such a small country, with hardly any natural resources could have become one of the most powerful countries in the world for a few centuries now?

Eventually I found the answer in a book describing the world development in the 19th century, a book clear and concise in actual facts and very little comment. It was a fascinating read describing the invention, the inventor and – let one's imagination run with the facts – *no* propaganda. At the time everything had been invented by a Russian, usually an uneducated peasant from the Urals and the stories were embellished with such ridiculous claims that nobody, especially I, believed a word of it! But this book of inventors and inventions had the whiff of truth and reality and I started counting up the list of one hundred most important inventions for humanity: penicillin was a very good example –it gave everybody on earth an extra twenty years of life on average and the British person who discovered it did not want to take a patent that most likely would have made him the richest person on earth and I was truly impressed, so much so that I even memorised the date Professor Alexander Fleming discovered penicillin: it was the morning of Friday 28th September 1928, a date very much worth remembering; at that time.

I was hardly aware of the different nations that make up Great Britain and I called everyone English; one of the first mistakes to correct when I came to London many years later.

The list of top one hundred inventions / innovations had no fewer than 62 made by the British, from No. 2 Electricity (No. 1 was the printing press, by a German), No. 3 Penicillin, No. 8 vaccination, followed by the steam engine, and so on. There are many things that will excite a teenager's mind, and that of being an inventor excited me most. I dreamt a great deal about it, many, many dreams, nothing concrete until I decided that what really needed a radical change was obviously in physics (my weakest subject in school, the only one I had less than maximum mark, much to my deep annoyance). For a start, if we already knew all the laws of Physics – and those laws are what they are meant to be – how come that mankind keeps inventing things that contradict most of those very laws? On a personal basis I had my first brush with the laws of physics and their marvellous formulas with my own early experience.

At the time I was twelve and it was the worst part of my life by far. My father 'existed' no more, mother was still in jail and I was at the mercy of strangers. For water I would use a well with a bucket, a chain and a wheel. To get water I'd drop the bucket in the well and then I'd start pulling the chain that was going through a wheel above my head, and that was that. Come the Physics lesson and I was presented with a formula which told me that I was doing it wrong because I was wasting extra energy due to the friction between the chain and the guiding wheel. Hang on, I thought, I don't believe this. This formula is nice, reasonable, impressive and obviously rubbish when tested. I could hardly wait for the school day to end and then I went straight to the water well and did my own experiment. Little did I know what an unexpected and extraordinary effect this would have on my future. I started by pulling buckets of water first without using the wheel and I managed to do twelve before I was exhausted; it was a very deep well. To maintain scientific parity between the two tests, I waited several hours before I did the second part of the test, pulling down the chain with the bucket using the wheel. Net result, I managed to pull twenty-two buckets before feeling any tiredness, almost double what the scientific formula was telling me was the right way, friction and all! After this experiment I was left extremely wary about any formula that did not take account of what I call 'the human factor' – of course I quickly realised that for humans it is much easier to pull down than to pull up! Still, this little experiment had other unforeseen consequences as far as I was concerned. Using the water in the well as my experimental laboratory did not go down very well with the neighbours who had to wait for hours for the waters in the well to replenish and the mud to settle down; they promised me in no uncertain terms a good thrashing if I ever did it again, and they meant it.

After that experiment I declared to myself that modern physics had more to do with black magic than with any reality. At sixteen I wrote a short paper on the subject and I declared clearly and for everyone to read that Newton was right and that Einstein was just an overhyped charlatan by comparison – his theory of relativity was nothing but a theory and to state that nothing could travel faster than the speed of light was surely barmy and contradicted the day to day reality. Gravity, according to Newton (and me, obviously!), has infinite speed, which stands to reason; the universe wouldn't hang in one piece without gravity that holds it together, and given the immensity of the universe the speed of gravity *has* to be infinite, what could be simpler? I was a Newtonian, through and through, and very grateful for that. I stated as much in my paper and in true Christian tradition I wrote my scientific essay by hand and stapled it to the door of the Head of School. Big, big mistake! My *Scientific Pamphlet* to give it its original title expressed a sort of revolutionary zeal and contradicted in a way the communist all powerful dogma. It wasn't long before somebody notified the secret police about this 'counter-revolutionary' paper and I was promptly arrested and interrogated for many weeks as a counter-revolutionary at the secret police headquarters.

The comrade interrogators were not exactly up to date with the sophisticated sciences; one of them was convinced that this character Newton must have been a contact abroad, plotting the overthrow of the people's paradise; it stood to reason, Newton was an English name was it not? The other comrade interrogators were not exactly the fastest trains out of the depot either. All they wanted to know was who else was part of this anti-revolutionary conspiracy and beat the hell out of me to tell them who they were. Under torture I still wasn't able to tell them anything, and I lost a kidney in the process.

I was eventually released when the Chief interrogator learned from somewhere that 'comrade Einstein' was 'one of us', in the same class as Marx and Engels and so my case was dropped. I was packed up and taken to a military hospital for treatment and recuperation! I underwent major surgery at the military facility to remove the kidney damaged during the interrogations and for some bizarre reason (even by the comrade's standards) I was given electric shocks at the back of my head which resulted in me losing my hair earlier than anyone else in my family. This experience, if anything, made me a great deal more determined in my scientific endeavours. The fact that the comrades were so scared by my ideas, convinced me that I was right – such a lovely feeling – and that the comrades, as usual, were completely wrong. (What a shame that they were the ones in power!) Strangely enough, despite the 'small mishaps of my encounters' with the *Stasi* (State Security Service), my scientific endeavours saved me at that time from a much worse future.

Acquaintances of mine had set up an illegal political organisation with the aim of overthrowing the regime, but I was following my own path and just ignored them. It turned out to be a very wise thing to do. One of them betrayed the rest and all ended up in jail, sentenced for twenty years or so. Out of twelve just two 'made it' and were released after the 'comrades' communist heaven' collapsed in 1989 to the delight of most people – the joke went like this: *We'd all been waiting for the collapse of communism, had fought for it all our lives and guess what, the communists beat us to it, bastards, they destroyed it themselves! Real evil people!*

Canvassing for Labour

The political scene of the 1980s in Britain was anything but a boring one, Mrs Thatcher having her own personal way of winning almost everything. We'd decisively won the Falklands war, to my enormous delight and satisfaction – I was glued to the radio and TV non-stop and I was physically sick when a British ship was sunk by the cowardly Argentinians and many British sailors died; I was so passionate that I even had a physical 'argument' in a pub with a guy I'd never met before who was advocating no more, no less the abandonment of the Falklands to the Argentinians – net result I lost a tooth during the 'argument' but Britain defeated the Argentinians and the British nation (most of it anyway), took to heart Mrs Thatcher's advice and 'rejoiced'! So did I and I felt very proud about it!

With her political powers greatly enhanced by her firm attitude and action against the 'invading Argies', Mrs Thatcher then proceeded to privatise the rather sclerotic previously nationalised industries, fought a long battle with the striking miners and won it, and to crown it all she won the next election with an even greater majority, while the opposition was divided and the Labour party were busily writing their 'new manifesto' also known as 'the longest suicide letter in history'! The 1980s was the time of 'lots of money' and 'Tell Sid' slogans, 'everybody' making lots of money to the despair of the many people left out who sincerely and deeply hated *that bloody woman*! And they were not the only ones. Believe it or not, when the IRA failed in their attempt to assassinate Mrs Thatcher, I was horrified to hear some 'natives' of Chelsea, pretty close neighbours of hers, making comments along the lines of 'what a pity they missed' – it might have been the famous British sense of humour brought to its absolute limits, or perhaps they had really meant it! Little did I know then that those who would eventually assassinate her politically, were in her own close circle, those she trusted most and fully relied on.

In 1987 it was clear that she'd win the coming general election again hands down as they say, or by a country mile (whatever that is!). This rather unchallenging election I decided, would be a good test for me in my quest of becoming what Merry called 'more British than the British' and in true British fashion I started fighting, gallantly, for a lost cause and campaigned for The Labour Party – in Chelsea of all places! Of course Merry thought the idea was 'a hoot' and Ben, despite nearing his sixth form exams decided to join 'the labour mini-campaign' and offered straight away his services in placing red 'Vote Labour' flyers under the windscreen wipers of any Rolls Royce, Aston Martin or Jaguar parked south of King's Road, all the way to Gloucester Road, quite a few of them! The area encompasses The Boltons, huge villas with even bigger gardens, the biggest in Central London after Buckingham Palace, conveniently placed a few dozen yards distance from Drayton Gardens which gave me a feeling of adventure and, why not, achievement! There is a Square in Chelsea with fourteen houses, and from the previous electoral role list, the lowest title in this area was that of 'sir'. There were also assorted 'princes', lords and the like and I approached the first door with a reasonable amount of trepidation.

I rang the bell, and the door was opened by a gentleman whom I took to be the owner, in fact it was only the butler. I explained the reason for my visit, handed him a couple of leaflets extolling the benefits of a Labour Government for the working class and prepared to leave when I heard a voice inviting me to the smoking room where I had the pleasure of explaining to Sir Nicholas why he should consider voting Labour. He listened to my deeply felt passion in pleading the labour cause without interrupting and then asked if I liked a cup of tea or coffee? No, I didn't as I had already spent almost all the time I'd allocated myself for 'convincing' everybody in the square. Before I left, Sir Nicholas assured me that he would "bear in mind the advantages of a Labour government" and we parted on the best of terms. The next imposing villa was an almost carbon copy of my first encounter as were the last three villas I managed to get through the first door.

Half encouraged by their promises I decided to do a bit of canvassing in the furthest corner of Chelsea, rather appropriately named The World's End, the poorest part of the Royal Borough and where there are several tower blocks which were built for the poor of the borough during a previous Labour Government in their efforts for a mixed society – just to spite the local aristocracy. Very nice flats too, very well located and now all property of the original tenants, thanks to Mrs Thatcher's right to buy policy (of selling the council's flats at a ridiculously low price!). This must be Labour territory I reasoned and, full of new enthusiasm, knocked at the first door and started my spiel:

"Good evening sir, I am here on behalf of The Labour Party," I addressed the half-naked guy, who seemed to have just got out of bed.

"Oh, *get lost!*" and he banged the door shut with so much disgust that the hall reverberated. Definitely not a Labour supporter! Next door was even less encouraging; the person at the door mentioned some acts of aggression he would subject me to if I ever knocked at his door again. Things got even worse a few doors up and I started to wonder if this was the best place for my canvassing. Dark thoughts of lack of gratitude or loyalty towards crowded my mind.

At last at one door I got a sympathetic hearing. The gentleman, although smelling heavily of alcohol was more or less up-to-date with the political events in the country at that time; he even remembered vaguely that there was something called elections coming soon, definitely in the future! After a few minutes in which I explained carefully all the benefits coming his way if only he would bother to vote the right way, i.e. Labour, I got a positive and enthusiastic reply

"Of course I shall vote for Labour," he gladly reassured me. And then he confirmed it once more, "I love that woman, what's her name, yes Mrs Thatcher, I shall definitely vote for her and the Labour!"

Oh dear, I put him as a 'maybe'. Just before leaving the tower block, I stopped at the penthouse flat door and tried my luck, for one last time. Rang the bell, door opened and a fearsome looking creature greeted me with an inquisitive look.

"On behalf of the Labour Party," I started in a polite manner, but it didn't work.

"Fuck off!" was the unfriendly greeting before the door was closed and firmly locked. I felt completely dejected. However, being sworn at upset me even more than the lack of support for the Labour Party – nobody had ever sworn at me in Chelsea before and I suddenly doubted the wisdom of building houses for people who shouldn't really be allowed to 'inhabit' *my* beloved Chelsea!

Back in Drayton Gardens I told Merry the details of my electoral exploits! I explained how mystified I was at the way people reacted to my well-meaning efforts. How baffling the behaviour of the voters in the Boltons had been and especially the attitude of those "ungrateful idiots" in the World's End tower blocks. Merry had a good laugh, opened a bottle of decent red wine (we had started to drink quite a lot together at that time) and proceeded to explain where I had gone wrong, how and why.

"Look, the people in Boltons will never vote Labour, if their lives depended on it. There is a better chance you'll be the next Emperor of China than they will change their minds; and they did their best to waste your canvassing time pretending they might be interested. Come on Michael, you must have learned by now that if someone around here says 'I'll bear it in mind' that is as good as saying 'forget it'. Besides, nobody is that naïve to believe promises made during electoral campaigns – there's a limit to any democracy, including ours, let's be realistic."

What was realistic just then was that Merry was drinking too much, too much for my liking or for health and looks. Perhaps I should have had a chat with her about it, but I'd do it after the elections!

But she hadn't finished her explanation for my rather unsuccessful foray into front line politics.

"As for the World's End lot, what do you expect?" she asked. "Mrs Thatcher has bought them all for generations by selling them very valuable properties all over the country at ridiculously low prices. You and I and everyone else knows that there is nothing more precious in this country than having your own house. Remember the saying that one man's home is another man's castle? – that is the way it is. It is Mrs Thatcher's rather smart policies that have transformed those people, the mass of former tenants, into homeowners for the first time in their families' history almost overnight. You see, the Labour party built the houses for the poor so more people became council tenants; then Mrs Thatcher came and more or less 'gave away' those flats to the tenants. Who would *you* vote for, then?" And then she cheerfully helped herself to yet another glass of wine.

Oh, not another glass, I had better take the bloody bottle away. I took a long, deep breath and changed the subject and brought some good news.

TransManche Link (TML project)

"You must have heard me and others talking about this new project, the Channel Tunnel, running into more and more difficulties with the works going nowhere and the banks threatening to cut any future financing, or to pull the plug which I think is the correct expression. It is only the ensuing embarrassment at the highest level of having to abandon the much vaunted project that keeps it going but it will not last for long. It is of course more of a vanity project for Mitterrand, the French President, but it is a matter of national pride and prestige for Britain and Mrs Thatcher personally. Something has to be done to keep the project going, better still put it on a firm holding and have it complete, whatever the cost…"

"Oh yes, of course darling," Merry muttered half asleep.

"I've been approached and asked if I could come up with a project control system that will convince the extremely sceptical banks to continue financing the project showing realistically the true cost and timescale, defining a precise ending in sight." I looked at Merry totally asleep now and for the first time I heard her snoring, a loud penetrating noise, extremely annoying. But I carried on, mainly for my own benefit!

"I said yes, based mainly on what I've learned from Shell Expro and all the other oil and gas companies in the North Sea. The North Sea is perhaps the hardest place on earth to extract oil and gas, the standard of technical work is second to none, if anything many years ahead of the much simpler and easier 'land based' projects. I could apply sophisticated methods calculating all construction activities in a manner that civil engineering cannot even dream of!"

I've always been suspicious of civil engineering; it hasn't

changed much in the last three thousand years or so, except it's become more and more profligate with its costs and expenses!

"I shall use the latest methods, the most advanced computer methods and come up with an agreed method for pricing and timing this particular project. I shall use the Critical Path method, invented, believe it or not, by the guys who built the Polaris submarines in the US."

At that time, to build a Polaris Submarine required over five million independent activities, an absolute nightmare unless one used the Critical Path method. In other words you do away with the situation where you have 'too many priests but no holy book' – all I was asked was to produce a 'holy book' good enough for the bankers to release money!

"I calculate that the Channel Tunnel will have less than a million activities to be dealt with, Terminals included – a real piece of cake! I am on! Of course I shall also use a system called CTR (Cost Time Resources) which should please the bankers no end – it is in fact the golden principle, a lock if you want. There can't be an activity without a cost or any cost without an activity. Simple!"

Finally, I let Merry sleep on the sofa in her alcoholic stupor and I went to sleep alone in the music room.

The TML project went smoothly, thanks to my CTR system in the main, but I couldn't expect gratitude from the French Partners, all ten companies of them who promptly tried to take the credit for the success, each and every one. But I wasn't going to let them get away with that one. Smartly, I kept a copy of my final issue of the system for constructing TML and I had it available for inspection, when required!

Thomas and modern art

It may sound slightly strange, but at the time there seemed to be some sort of symbiotic link between the bankers and the well to do aristocrats of Chelsea and politically left-wing intellectuals from the northern parts of London, places like Islington, the posher side, and the hilly side of Hampstead. Merry always liked to have the intellectual or artistic representatives of the left at her dinner parties and in truth, it did make for very fine and sophisticated entertainment. I greatly enjoyed one hundred per cent every minute of those parties, so much so that I started preparing and offering some obscure *Oversylvanian* dishes, 100% vegetarian and obviously politically correct, within limits. The dishes I prepared were very tasty, apparently. I might as well try them myself one day!

There was a sort of ritual for Merry and her inner circle of friends, some very interesting people, in the way the dinner party circuit was organised; it took place routinely in The Royal Borough with the odd 'adventure' in nearby Belgravia and in exceptional cases the 'party circus' ventured as far as Hampstead. It took hours and hours to drive across London to the place and, even Islington (been there twice in ten years!). I give Merry full credit for her circle, 'a motley crew', I once heard some pretentious guy comment dismissively, but for me they were all extremely interesting; they were as a rule, actors, dancers, artists; mainly people who were always on TV in different guises. Later I found out that for a short period Merry had been the Culture Editor of one of the most important daily newspapers in the UK. Her father was a famous painter, by the way, famous for more than just painting as it happens! Merry's estranged husband Bill had by that time become an admired writer by those who really understood literature – apparently reading a book and sometimes understanding it, is nowhere near enough – and his much younger Australian secretary who admired Bill so much so that they lived together. However, the Australian secretary was somehow never invited.

I still wonder if Merry ever divorced Bill; apparently there were complicated financial arrangements to be dealt with and Merry never liked to talk about her personal 'mess'. "Too boring darling!" to talk about, "let's have another drink!" was her way of fobbing off any delicate questioning. Asking personal questions, especially those of a financial nature, was not the 'done thing' in Britain, Chelsea anyway. I found out pretty quickly that it was normal for each party in a marriage to be perfectly ignorant of their spouse's income and general financial matters!

Merry never did sitting down parties; the 'routine' was always rather different, but any hostess in Chelsea then would have given anything for something new and attractive so the 'people that matter' would talk about it. It depended on who you had on your list and even more importantly who'd been invited not only as a guest but also as a performer. Being *it*, preferably an internationally renowned musician or a famous choreographer, London with its vibrant musical scene was a rewarding goldmine in this respect. Robin, a former dancer and a splendid choreographer was one of Merry's favourites, although due to his contacts at the time was hardly available because, as he used to explain, "you know darling, the *Royals*, I wouldn't say which one, you understand of course, they are *ever* so demanding so I couldn't possibly disappoint them. I have no time at all, I am on permanent call, the phone may ring any minute now, I really I must dash!"

Showing off was de rigueur amongst most of Merry's circle, although there was also Ron L, the Vice President of a huge Multinational Company, a 'fat cat' as the left-wing papers would have it or a very "smart cookie" as Merry used to say. I ended up being quite close to Ron given the fact that we played tennis together, and I always made sure (well, almost always) that Ron won the final set, which greatly pleased him and also greatly amused me – at that time his company employed tens of thousands of people, had a turnover of many billions of pounds and Ron would jump up and down with joy after winning a poncey tennis match with some obscure refugee! Well, perhaps not so obscure as things turned out.

A collection of two dozen or so of the great and good would gather, and with plenty of drinks, mainly champagne to start with, and all sorts of vol au vents and easy snacks, caviar and vodka, things always went smoothly. I must admit, never mind how tired or indisposed she might have been, Merry would always be the soul and the burning flame of her parties. There was no such thing as a boring dinner party as far as Merry was concerned and, come what may, she'd be there, the life, the soul and the spirit of the party. She made sure that everything was in its right place before the first guest arrived, all guests were amazingly punctual as in Chelsea it was 'not the done thing' to be late, whoever you were.

I was always the one to help serve the drinks as Merry wouldn't have 'outside help'; we were very much against exploitation and the like and besides, having strangers overhear our conversations was a no-no! I must admit I learned a great deal about drinks and how to serve them since my student days and my job as a barman!

This sort of party with its carefully selected 'by chance' cast of participants worked extremely well with a well-established ritual. Of course, talking politics was not done but complaining loudly about that 'bloody woman' was! Of course, that 'bloody woman' was Mrs Thatcher, and almost all guests would pile in with their horror stories about 'that woman'. I still find it hard to understand how many people despised her although if I understand correctly she made most people in Chelsea much richer through her policies – not much of a thank you by any standards. Their main complaint (if that is the right word) about Mrs Thatcher was not the fact that she originated from somewhere up north (Grantham, I think, but for most of Merry's guests anything north of Oxford Street was 'up north' and better ignored!). The assembled congregation, as I liked to refer to them, was in agreement that Mrs Thatcher was "the biggest social climber since Cinderella" which I still find absolutely hilarious! They had (and still have) a way with words in Chelsea! Eventually, when everybody had had quite a bit to say and drink came the part that fascinated me most; observing and talking about the guests.

There was Thomas, a recent graduate of The Royal Academy of Art, at the top of the class and already an artist 'to watch', especially since he had decided to give up conventional painting and intended switching to 'installation works', things like unmade beds, pickled sharks, that sort of thing. "Everybody is into that nowadays, that is where the money is," he would state proudly. Thomas was not only a talented painter in conventional terms (in my view someone capable of mixing more than two colours; as for the more 'modernist' lot who just splash one colour on canvas and charge astronomically! – personally I think it is all a big swindle but I'm not going to feel sorry for the people who buy the stuff, bankers and financial advisers (whatever they are) mainly because they know all about crap and how much to invest in the crap of their choice!) Thomas was extraordinarily good looking, which added to my slight unease; it was really too much for a man! Still, he was always invited, mainly on the strength of his good looks, painting talent and uncompromising opinions, strictly in that order. And he always turned up with the most gloriously looking young lady who was always draped, there is no other word, around his neck, cuddling and kissing him non-stop to the dismay of the ladies of a certain age who suddenly showed a great deal of interest in this new 'art' installation; whatever Thomas was into, they would be there too! Obviously Thomas despised art dealers and loudly declared that they were all leeches, including a couple present (quite decent and pleasant chaps actually, of Armenian origin as it happened.) They were highly regarded in their business for their honesty and reliability but that was no impediment for Thomas to keep whispering "leeches" in their direction and inbetween dealing with the never-ending kisses from his latest faiblesse, still wrapped firmly around his neck.

I found Thomas's painting a bit 'iffy'. Merry commissioned him to produce a painting of me, full size and with masses of colours – this idea satisfied the highest level of my ever-expanding vanity and pleased me no end to start with! I was prepared for multiple sittings but these never materialised – Thomas set me down on an armchair, told me to relax and took about a dozen photographs of me with different expressions and in different positions, and that was that. Thomas declared himself satisfied with the photos and disappeared for several weeks, keeping in touch just to ask for yet another advance and eventually he announced the grand presentation of what he declared was to be his last painting as he was moving to a new art form, *installations* for those in the know! Merry jumped for joy at the news and held a party for the unveiling of Thomas's 'last' painting.

Was he going to do the honourable thing and stop painting? Ron wondered. Ron's company had in the past commissioned Thomas to produce a series of paintings for the company's headquarters at Blackfriars Bridge which Thomas did in record time and for an exorbitant price. However Ron declared the paintings "ghastly" and instead of exhibiting them in The Grand Marble Hall of the very imposing company headquarters, had them demoted to the staff canteen with the net result that nobody hung around in the canteen at lunch for very long!

Merry pulled out all the stops (I'm learning new expressions every day!) and managed to even invite someone from Vogue, God only knows why; I was not male model material by any stretch of the imagination, but being 'a scientist' was something that the Chelsea lot didn't encounter every day although Dr Fleming, of penicillin discovery fame, had once lived in Chelsea, blue plaque to prove it. Anyway, the gathering was impressive even by Merry's highest standards and everybody waited for Thomas and 'my' painting. Thomas turned up in what I was told was his 'traditional style' – only one hour late. This time he'd brought two admirers with him to carry the full size painting to the first floor flat. He made a grand entrance gesture and started by what I took to be swearing, not totally unexpected, but on examination I discovered he was a reciting a poem in Welsh, written by himself as he rather modestly and dead drunk admitted later.

The two young ladies unveiled the painting, everyone applauded, the other ladies gave deep sighs of satisfaction and something that can only be described as an artistic orgasm blossomed on their discreetly made up cheeks. I looked at the painting which to me seemed to be the Portrait of a Young Man by Holbein meets The Clocks by Salvador Dali, that Spanish surrealist painter with the strange moustache. There was I, like some young noble amongst magnificently exotic plants on some uninhabited landscape, dressed in some sort of rich and heavy bath robe with weird inscriptions. Of course I expressed my full satisfaction and happiness with the painting, which frankly was a bit of a disappointment. However, the painting was somehow mollified by the beauty of one of the girls holding it. I suddenly became interested in that beautiful girl and I exchanged a few banalities with her in a dialogue that did not go very well.

"Do you like the painting?" I asked her.

"Oh, this one?" she replied aloof. "Frankly, I did not have a look at it, I am just doing a job, carrying it."

What, a young lady with such extraordinary looks and she is temping carrying some stupid painting around.

As if she'd read my thoughts she added,

"I am a student and I need to earn some money, we don't all live in Chelsea you know. I'll give you my card before I go. If you have any odd jobs, waitressing, things like that, give me a call. I do house cleaning as well."

I was just about to say, you must stay a bit longer, have a drink and relax a bit, when Merry intervened.

"Thank you darling, you are such a sweetie, now we'll just put the painting in the hall temporarily and ... good night." She almost pointed to the door to this, *the most beautiful young creature I'd ever seen*, the nearest beauty to Botticelli's Venus. There was no doubt in my mind that one of the ancestors of this present day Venus must have been Botticelli's model.

Merry took her card, said indifferently, "we'll keep in touch" and the most beautiful creature floated down the stairs and disappeared towards Gloucester Road. Ron, who must have been watching the scene, came up with a glass of champagne and after Merry left said,

"Beautiful one isn't she?"

"Who are you talking about?" I professed total innocence rather unconvincingly.

"Fabienne, that is her name, she is a French student at the Royal College of Music, if you want to know. But you'll be wasting your time, she is not the type."

"Never mind who she is, if I see her again OK, if not, so be it. What do you think about the painting anyway?"

"Absolute crap," was Ron's unbiased opinion expressed in a direct language. "I hope you haven't paid him the full price; it needs a great deal more work."

"Well, I have actually, but you are right; I'd want him to modify a thing or two."

"Don't," was Ron's advice, "he'll charge you the full amount again. I've done business with Thomas before, you watch it. Let's hope he keeps his promise and gives up painting for the sake of all of us including him!"

"Yes, Ron, he is clearly no painter but why do so many people in the know buy his paintings? He's not cheap by any means. All these dealers cannot all be blind?" I reasoned with Ron.

"Oh no, they're not blind, believe it or not they are the smartest creatures around and Thomas, despite all his bravado and bohemian behaviour, is a painter with modest talent but great personality and phenomenal good looks. He is a marketing tool, an ideal marketing tool, he has a 'great name' peddled all over Mayfair galleries, the people with money, the bankers in the City who can't tell the difference between graffiti and Michelangelo, buy anything that their art dealer in Mayfair advises is a great investment to have. There is a symbiotic relationship between the 'artist' and the money men, well functioning, well oiled and, most importantly, well protected. Not much is left to chance. The Art gallery and the City institutions have a perfect system of fooling one another and as long as nobody rocks the boat, we are all happily floating in the air! Personally, I am investing in this new thing called installations, before the prices go through the roof. Thomas is smart, he's got no artistic talent and installations are designed for the likes of him. Besides, as painting has become more and more childish, it is easier to counterfeit and frankly, they say that over eighty per cent of all Picasso's and other such works are all counterfeits."

I looked at Ron in disbelief.

"You are not serious, it just cannot be true, as much as *that?*"

"I tell you a true story," he said topping his glass with whisky, "I know it from my father who was a keen collector in the fifties and knew almost every art dealer in Mayfair. Picasso, that is *the* Picasso, used to come to London pretty often to see his personal art dealer in Dover Street, the most respected dealer in London and do some casual shopping. This one time his dealer produced what he presumed was a painting by Picasso but which unfortunately the artist had forgotten to sign.

'I'm sorry to trouble you but can you please sign it, it was bought by one of our American clients and she would like you to sign it, it is for her collection,' he gently prompted Picasso.

Picasso carefully examined the painting and declared:

'This is not by me, definitely not mine.'

The dealer went white faced and pleaded

'Oh dear, if that is the case I shall have to return our client her money and she is going to be very unhappy. She has been one of our clients for a very long time, shame but what can I do?' the dealer almost burst into tears.

'How good a client is she?' Picasso interrupted.

'Oh, she's a very, *very* good client,' the dealer confirmed enthusiastically!

'Good, then the painting is by me,' Picasso relented and promptly signed it!'' Ron concluded.

Bang went another little illusion about the value of art. Mind you I never really liked Picasso to start with and now I had my little satisfaction! Perhaps the paintings I'd been told were by Picasso are in fact just forgeries, there must be a real Picasso somewhere that would prove if he was the great painter everyone 'in the know' enthuses about. I thought, if I am lucky I'll find it one day!

Meanwhile, I found myself thinking of Fabienne – what a beautiful name – and I wondered if I'd see her again. I thought Ron must surely know more about her and Merry didn't like her much. There was no question of me having any sort of physical relationship with Fabienne, I was too lazy and too vain to go chasing a nubile young lady and frankly, cheating was not really my style, I reassured myself trying to go to sleep while Merry who had been drinking a fair amount felt unwell and was twisting and turning in bed. She decided eventually to ring her mother and then spent at least half an hour describing in minute detail the "beautiful party" she'd just hosted, but she didn't mention Fabienne, thank God!

Eventually, I fell asleep and I had an extraordinary dream.

It was the Middle Ages and I was in Rome, in the papal Palace in the Vatican, no less, and I was witness to a discussion between the Pope, a very imposing gentleman looking more like a military conqueror than a spiritual leader, and an elderly painter-cum-decorator who was being given instructions how to paint the ceiling of this new extension to the papal Palace. The gentleman in military attire was Pope Julius II and the labourer was a chap known as Michelangelo, a sculptor and architect, but in my dream the Pope was ordering him to paint the ceiling of the Sistine Chapel, a work that would take a long, long time to complete, about five years was Michelangelo's rough estimate. The fresco was to be called The Last Judgement but Michelangelo would rather not do it, too much hassle and he was more a sculptor than painter/decorator and anyway, painting was so 'yesterday', nowadays it was all about 'installations'. *"Believe you me, man,"* Michelangelo pleaded with the Pope, *"installation is cool, man."*

An exasperated Pope asked

"But what *is* an installation?"

"Now you're talking," replied Michelangelo. "Look, if you want more people to get your message, installation is the answer. Put an unmade bed in the middle of the Sistine Chapel and the faithful, terminally naïve will queue around the corner to stare and wonder in disbelief at this marvel of human civilisation! *You cannot go wrong, man!* Alternatively, you could leave my scaffolding in place and the way mankind is going all art critics will praise the scaffolding and damn the paintings which are a bit overdone anyway!"

* * *

The following morning while in a hurry to leave the flat for a walk on Chelsea embankment, my daily physical exercise, I couldn't stop thinking about the previous night. First of all that good-looking fraud masquerading as a painter or whatever he now called himself 'creator of installations'; *creator* no less – he and God Almighty! Still, bloody Thomas must have been nearly thirty and he had the skin of a child. I wondered what creams he was using to keep his bloody skin and features in such good shape despite his let's call it 'unconventional' lifestyle! I came eventually to the only reasonable conclusion: perhaps I too would have such a perfect skin, velvety and clean, like the skin of an early ripe peach, if I too were being kissed non-stop by the most beautiful women around. To add to my chagrin I could not stop thinking that Thomas must be painting some of those exquisite looking creatures in the nude!

It took a great deal of self-convincing that envy is the only vice with no profit or pleasure, easier said than done, but finally I settled on asking for Fabienne's telephone number, but he fobbed me off. He'd put it somewhere but couldn't remember where – Bastard!

Hm, something to ponder upon!

About 'my painting', I still have it somewhere among my long-term storage belongings. Somehow, I never looked at it after parting from Merry. I have a photo of it somewhere handy, just in case! It should have been an installation, after all!

Merry's goodbye

The summer of 1988 was a glorious time, at least as far as I was concerned. First, Ben got his A levels with maximum marks, somewhat to my surprise and a very pleasant surprise at that. Now Ben could apply for a place at Imperial College if he so wished or any other prestigious university but to my further surprise Ben, who'd just got a new girlfriend, also a dedicated 'biker', had decided to move out and live with her in some poncey place in Notting Hill Gate. (Love is not only blind but inconvenient as well at the best of times.) Ben moved out all his motorbike bits and pieces from the balconies, to our neighbours' delight and general well-meant good wishes – they also appreciated the disappearance of Ben's biker friends, about twelve of them at the final count!

Ben during his teenage years had been what can only be described as a model teenager, so much so that at times I wondered if he was hiding something important from Merry and I – 'you know how teenagers are', the saying goes. Not this one! He had developed into an eighteen-year-old of over six foot without giving us the slightest worry about his general well-being; no smoking, no drinking and no question of drugs. Always a diligent and well behaved young man, except that is for wearing biker leather outfits and identitkit girls dressed in similar attire! I never realised how many of those teenage girls with the most extraordinary skin texture and demure eyes would transform into something completely different the moment they dressed in leather, still beautiful but with extra personality projection that made them even more interesting. Altogether I cannot recollect one occasion when I had to lay down the law with Ben or even raise my voice to him when he might 'have forgotten' to do some of his homework. I didn't, there was no need!

By June 1988 I was in the position to submit the grandly named The Project System for TransManche-Link (TML) Operating Plan, or simply The Operating Plan, just on time for TML to convince the banks to pour several billion pounds more into the Channel Tunnel venture; my study was accepted without any modifications and I was very proud of it – I still keep one of the original copies for my own ego and pride. The time has been kind to what I consider a main part of my working life; the Channel Tunnel is working perfectly to this day and it will for decades to come; as a technical achievement it is up there with some of the greatest constructions in the world and if this is not fulfilling one's professional achievements, what else is there?

In fairness I must admit that producing the operating plan was a lot easier than most people expected. Essentially, all I had to do was apply, for the first time I think, the know-how from the North Sea oil and gas explorations to a civil construction and all its components. Of course I had to write solid reliable algorithm programmes; I could not afford the slightest mistake on this type of enterprise, and I was extra careful; but I *did* use a concept from my North Sea experience that I saw working in the most difficult and dangerous situations. I will not bore you with details, although I really wish I could, suffice to say the system works and many others followed.

Still, this nagging worry remained (albeit in a well hidden place): what do I do *next*? Not just for an encore but also for something much grander and more visionary than everything hitherto! My vanity, my best and worse characteristic at all times, just does not leave me alone. Problem is that I feel drained by satisfaction and incredibly proud of myself. I've even considered a hair transplant for the hair loss on the top of my head! Meanwhile, I've been using a French product that seems to be working; it's stopped me losing hair but I seem to have some curious heartbeats at times; I just wonder if there is a correlation.

* * *

The day before Ben left Drayton Gardens, Merry decided to make some sort of official statement of *'Thank You Michael for all you've done for Ben'* in a grand manner and with all the friends gathered together. It was impressive and highly emotional. Everybody applauded, congratulated me and got sloshed on the last few bottles of champagne and 'decent' wine left from the previous party. The party was kept secret from me but I found the surprise very rewarding. I almost burst into tears of gratitude but, as I learned, in the Anglo-Saxon world the man never cries, "it is not done" as Merry's mother would say, with her sternest intonation, no doubt!

I was so moved and so completely chuffed that I could not even open my mouth, a first! And I wandered almost aimlessly among the guests noticing things I had never really noticed about them before. There was Gayle, mainly unattached and on the lookout for the next 'great love' dressed in the latest designer outfit of some sort when in fairness all she needed was a tee shirt saying 'nothing to declare, all on display'! 'Bedroom eyes' and 'make love to me shoes' to match! There was Zeta of course and Ron, but not together as they were still divorcing but not quite there; they had their separate lives – and parties, obviously.

At the last one, given by Ron, with Zeta not invited, she turned up in the ballroom (they do have an impressive ballroom in their home) with the Philippine housekeeper in tow and an ironing board which she installed among the puzzled guests and then started ironing Ron's underwear ignoring everyone else. I don't know what other people would have done in such a situation, perhaps some physical force would have been appropriate in some other places but definitely not in Drayton Gardens, at any time. Later when the party was almost over, a dead drunk Ron made what I think was the greatest threat of his life:

"I shall I have bouncers at the door next time; someone must be able to stop this ghastly creature." I couldn't think of a better idea, shame he hadn't thought of it earlier in the day!

Back at Merry's party in my honour, Robin turned up late, as usual, and promptly informed everyone who cared to listen:

"Oh darlings, it is all *so* hectic. You know how the *Royals* are, you never have your own time," referring obviously to a certain princess, icon of elegance and beauty according to Robin, but just "a social climber" according to the older families in Chelsea whose favourite put down was something like

"Oh, we all know *The Spencers*, don't we?", and that would suffice!

But Robin was in the full flow of creative choreographic display and promptly jumped over chairs and precious antique recamier just to demonstrate the latest steps he'd just taught the princess.

"She is such a natural darling, it is amazing how quickly she learns new steps, you know she could have been a great ballerina, she has it in her."

Luckily Robin needed a bit of rest during which time he spotted "that gorgeous looking young man" in the hall, one of Ben's friends, and asked me

"Who is he?"

"Well, one of Ben's best mates." I muttered.

"He's *gorgeous*, isn't he?" Robin enthused.

"Yes, but you know he is a biker, a bit of a rough character, got a girlfriend biker as well!"

"Oh, how exciting," Robin's eyes suddenly lit by the elixir of desire. "I must talk to him. Better still, give him my telephone number and ask him to call me. I'd be interested, *very* interested!"

If only a small amount of the stories about Robin were anywhere near the truth. It was not the love of his life Robin was looking for, and somehow I didn't think Ben's friend would be interested, but then, who cares!

But there was more in store. A beautiful surprise for me was the presence of Fabienne … God she was beautiful. She seemed to have it all. She also had a ridiculous looking boyfriend in tow, but I didn't really care much. To see Fabienne and more importantly, to be able to talk to her freely and in a rather enthusiastic manner was such perfect joy. The joy like finding something you treasure, something you've thought you'll never see again, suddenly reappearing without warning or foresight. Fabienne and I seemed to have so much to talk about although we hardly knew one another – so much so that eventually Merry came across and suggested I get some more drinks for the guests, something she'd never done before. For the rest of the evening I felt Merry's eyes continuously following me around the place and I only spoke to Fabienne again when she left the party together with her precious boyfriend, some nondescript character, but her age and literally holding her hand.

Fabienne left, the lights dimmed, the last guests left the place reluctantly and slowly; the place quietened down to the relief of Mrs Wood in the flat below who didn't mind Merry's parties but she couldn't stand the noise they made, especially the dancing which apparently made her crystal chandeliers swing in a disturbing manner!

Talking to Merry before going to bed I casually remarked:

"They were a good mix, our guests, and they behaved … even Robin, a bit of a first!"

"Don't be so bitchy. Robin is a darling and an old dear friend. Ron and Zeta kept their distance thank God. They will explode one day, no doubt about that. Let's hope it is not going to happen in this place."

I smiled thinking that I wouldn't really mind seeing Zeta put in her precious place, and the sooner the better. However, I quickly changed the subject and complimented Merry on her choice of entertainment. We'd had Miss K. one of the greatest mezzo sopranos the stage has been blessed with; at that time semi-retired but still with the same powerful, multifaceted voice, unadulterated and almost painfully natural. Her rendition of Several Sons with just piano accompaniment was out of this world and Plaisir d'amour was extraordinarily moving and now I remember that Merry looked straight at me a couple of times while my eyes were wandering in a different direction. I didn't pay any notice at the time to such small details but they would prove to have more meaning than anything I ever expected.

Just before switching the lights off, I mentioned in a casual manner and smiling

"Did you invite that French girl, or did she just turn up, bit of a gate crasher?"

Merry knew exactly who the person in question was. She just said:

"She is such a beautiful girl, reminds me of the way I looked many years ago. And you know how much I like beautiful people around. The boyfriend she was with was very handsome as well."

"Do you mean she's got more than one boyfriend?" I found myself asking.

"My dear Michael, you are still so naïve. Someone as beautiful as Fabienne will always have a team of admirers, shall we say to be polite, and there will be, most likely, a full team of reserves, to speak in your sporting terms. Now good night," and Merry turned her back without kissing me good night, too exhausted perhaps after the long party. Later that night I thought I heard her gently weeping, but my desire to sleep was overwhelming and somehow, I could not imagine Merry crying.

* * *

How weather and things change before the midnight hour, how things turn in the most unexpected manner! A few days after my birthday in August Merry's mother was taken sick, very sick, and was hospitalised in St Mary's hospital in Paddington. Her luck, if that is the correct word, her proverbial 'luck' was by her side to the very end. Her heart gave up after two days and she was spared the thing she had feared most, that of a long and painful agony which was the only thing that most of the old people I'd met in Chelsea feared most, and that was easy to explain. Living a comfortable life and having the best medical care money can buy make the idea of physical pain a very distant and extremely unlikely occurrence as opposed to the place I came from where physical pain was an almost daily experience without any palliatives to hand except stoicism and the ability to curse one's bad luck!

Merry's mother had a peaceful passing away and a well prepared routine was put in place. While I dealt with the religious service at the church of her choice, I also dealt with the deeply unpleasant and gruesome details of having Merry's mother's body cremated. Merry insisted that it had been her mother's last wish and although uneasy about it, as a Christian belonging to the branch that believes deeply that you should be buried and never cremated, I had no choice. I made the necessary arrangements. Personally, though,

I'd rather be buried in a common grave or an unmarked one, but buried I must be!

I left aside the dark thoughts and slight forebodings, wishing them all away: 'I'll cross that bridge when I come to it' is the standard that I live my life now!

Merry also recovered pretty quickly from the shock of her mother's unexpected death and the business woman in her was in full flow yet again. Her mourning was rather short; there was a will to be dealt with, a very important will, as Merry's mother had been a lady with substantial assets in cash and property. To Merry's great relief she had left most of it to Merry, a good part to Ben and an acceptable amount to her few charities. I found myself smiling when she left nothing to me; I expected nothing and it only confirmed my deeply felt suspicion that she had never really accepted me, she had just tolerated me for the sake of Ben and Merry. Still she had been a shrewd woman who had protected what was left of her family and had done her best bequeathing them almost all her possessions.

Although, perhaps always expecting it, Merry found herself for the first time in her life, a woman of 'independent means'; lots of 'means' with independence to come!

During the years I lived with Merry, over ten years and counting, I did more than just pay my way. I paid all the bills and improved the place in Drayton Gardens with the latest hi-fi and imaginable TV equipment, and the odd painting or antique from Christie's. I was earning a great deal at the time so paying bills and the like was a matter of course. Same for Merry's parties, money was no object, although Merry was a much better 'accountant' than I would ever be!

True to form, Merry promptly let the first-floor flat overlooking Kensington Gardens, left to her with all its possessions by her mother, after first removing all the precious furniture and objects d'art and replacing the lot with stuff from Ikea. The flat looked empty and ugly but there were plenty of people competing to rent it. The rent from the flat plus a great deal of cash and jewellery left to Merry somehow changed the fine financial balance between me and Merry that had worked so well for years, but not anymore. With Ben gone as well, Merry found herself with a lot of time and money on her hands; shrewdly she knew how to deal with the financial part of it, but this time she left me out, and she dealt with everything herself. And there was something else. Robin, the choreographer, must have taken some time off from his 'royal engagements' at this time, enough to introduce Merry to some weird characters – 'mediums' – in Notting Hill Gate of all places.

Somehow, Robin's friends, the 'medium' lot discovered almost instantly that Merry was a 'natural medium', she really possessed 'the gift' and they made a great fuss about it. Of course, Merry adored her new friends which was sort of OK, but she trusted them, which was much more worrying. Merry used to pride herself on being a strong woman: she'd had to endure an errant husband who'd left her when she discovered she had breast cancer and as a result lost part of one of her breasts, a painful menopausal period; there were also bouts of depression (so common in women who could once stop the traffic with their looks alone, now slowly getting older and losing this most treasured asset, their looks).

There were so many evenings spent in, with me trying to convince her that she was as beautiful as ever, if not more so, carefully massaging her face and body with the latest exotic creams and oils, with mixed results, it must be said. I tried to help her expel her small demons by joining her in common wine evenings that over the years became more frequent. At the beginning of our relationship we had been perfectly happy to share one bottle of wine for the two of us; ten years late it had regularly reached a couple of bottles each and we were trying hard not to touch the hard spirits, pretty tempting at times. Our life was good but we were not well without even realising it. Still, the ending or dénouement (our downfall) came as a bolt from the blue, as far as I was concerned.

One evening in September, Merry was having one of her deep baths. She'd had one of the biggest baths I've ever seen installed in one of the bathrooms which she'd started to insist on having to herself, and I was allowed in only if Merry wanted a massage or 'better' and usually only after she'd finished the standard one bottle of wine, drunk from an enormous Jensen glass, so big as to take almost the whole bottle. "So," Merry would say with a satisfied smile, "I only drunk one glass darling!"

Usually, the call for my services would come at the end of the glass of wine, but this time she was in the bath, as usual full of colourful bubbles, but the customary glass of wine was untouched. Without looking at me, and before I'd even closed the bathroom door, Merry said in a simple, business-like manner

"I want to be on my own Michael. I want to split."

I was crestfallen. I thought I hadn't heard correctly what she'd said, or was she so drunk she was just talking nonsense? But Merry was never less drunk than on that day and for the first time in our relationship of over ten years she was suddenly changed into a cold and distant person. I never even suspected that she had it in her. Then Merry added in an even firmer tone

"I want us to separate and I want you out of here, the sooner the better. Now, please leave me alone and close the door."

It only took me a few minutes to realise that Merry was dead serious and that she wouldn't change her mind. First, I was absolutely furious, not with Merry, she was already the past, the 'wasted' past of my life and that was that. No, I was furious with myself for not having seen it coming. How could I have been so blind not to have noticed it? There must have been some signals of some sort. I am not a pub person, once or twice a year is more than enough for me, but that particular evening I needed a place to drink and think, or was it the other way round?

It was a Tuesday evening, a very quiet Tuesday evening and I got myself a corner place in the Drayton Arms and started drinking whisky, most unusual for me. Strange as it must sound but the whisky helped to clear my head and I started to reason. First question was obviously *what have I done to deserve it?* Nothing I could think of to start with. Never cheated on Merry, never been tempted even when some of her close friends had made it clear that they wouldn't mind a bit of rough; a close friend of hers even kept hinting at the enormous pleasure of 'threesomes', whatever they were, definitely *not* the thing to do in Chelsea.

OK, I liked this Fabienne, the French student but just from a distance; she was extremely beautiful but Merry was not bad despite her drunken wailings about being 'over the hill' – God, I do hate this expression, and me for giving her reassurances that it would never happen to her. So, what else was there for me but to be kicked out worse than you do to a dog? – I even smiled about it thinking that Merry couldn't legally have kicked a dog on the street. She would have been taken to court for cruelty to animals, whereas she was able to just kick me out at her pleasure – and some people would've applauded her for that! More whisky and the reality of what had happened started making sense, a great deal of sense.

The realisation that I had become 'surplus to requirements', hit me hard between my eyes; it explained everything. As far as Merry was concerned my usefulness had gone. Ben had finished his schooling, had transformed without any hiccups into a proud and decent person, and that was what the Thank You Michael party had been for. Merry was now a real wealthy person so my 'economic contribution' was no longer required either – just as well as recently my little business venture of importing wine had collapsed and I had lost a substantial amount of my savings in the process. The influence of her latest friends and her belief of being a medium and in constant communication with her deceased mother who 'advised her' from the other world, no less, must have had a strong bearing on her decision to kick me out; there was no other way of expressing it, Chelsea behaviour or not!

Right, enough of feeling sorry for myself! My mind was clear despite the entire whisky intake and I knew exactly what I had to do. First and foremost, I had to show dignity, be calm and understanding, after all, why not? If that was what it took to please Merry, so be it. But her decision had already killed something in me. The physical desire for her body had simply evaporated and I felt a strange sense of relief. I went to sleep in the main bedroom on the 'designer' futon, on my usual left side without talking or touching Merry. To my surprise I slept well and next morning we agreed that I should need a few weeks to sort out my stuff and find a reasonable place to live. Merry meanwhile would deal with what I called the logistics of our parting, or something on those lines.

It was a bit embarrassing dealing with legal matters, who owned what and the like, as we both had the same lawyer, the music lover Mr Isaacs, a person I greatly admired and respected instinctively. Merry presented me with a one page list for me to sign two days later, the day I was telephoned from *Oversylvania* and told that my mother had passed away. That hurt, it hurt a lot and then it hurt even more.

I couldn't go to the funeral to say the final goodbye, I would have been arrested or worse the moment I stepped onto *Oversylvanian* soil, still under communist rule. My mother's unexpected death numbed my senses and all dealings with Merry became superfluous and totally irrelevant. Although I'd spent a relatively short time with my mother in her life I learned from her perhaps the best quality one must acquire, that of dignity. I had lived with my mother through dreadful times under the communist regime; my father, a former high-ranking officer with impeccable military behaviour became an official 'enemy of the people' after the war and was executed after a standard communist show trial. My mother was also sent to prison for seven years for physically attacking the judge after the trial after which I'd only get to see her once every two months for a few minutes when I was allowed to deliver a small parcel with some food, mainly stolen. I only spent five or six years with my mother but her way of being put in me the essence of dignity. And she was the only person who knew about my plans of running away from the dictatorship's heaven to somewhere where I'd be judged according to my talents and contribution and not to who my parents were. I had her picture in my mind and I went and cried for hours in Kensington Gardens on an unusual October sunny day.

I signed and agreed with everything Merry put in front of me completely indifferent to what the conditions were. I had already decided in minute detail what the future, *my* future, would be like and there was not the slightest place for Merry. In fairness, Merry did agree to a financial arrangement in which I was given a certain amount of money as my share of the house in Marine Gardens in Kemptown, along with some other bits and pieces. Unfortunately, the list did not include all the common memorabilia, photos, video tapes and the like, they were all left with Merry and I was left with an empty gap of no memorabilia of my last ten years – it still feels strange at times, but it is one of those things, and that is that!

The last day for me in Merry's flat came to an even more abrupt end than I'd been expecting. Despite having set a day for me to leave at the weekend, she'd brought it forward to the Tuesday (apparently some medium had told her that this was the best day for her to kick me out) and she became so hysterical than I had no choice but to leave, with just a small suitcase, and take refuge in the penthouse flat on the top floor in the same block, where Rosemary, one of Merry's friends had a spare room.

I managed eventually to get most of my possessions from Merry's flat, courtesy of Rosemary's insistence mainly, a bit of an inconvenience but no more than that. One thing though, during the parting of ways between Merry and me, I didn't see or hear from Ben other than the one time I bumped into him, in a supermarket of all places! He looked and felt great and I was really happy and proud for him – I'd had something to do with his well-being and development; those years spent with him and Merry had not been a waste of time after all. And although I haven't seen or heard from Ben for three decades now, I still consider his upbringing a great success and something I am proud of. Of course, I have not seen or spoken to Merry since October 1988 and I have no intention of changing that. I saw someone the other day in King's Road who reminded me of her, she had some of her features but time had been unkind to her body. It might have been her, but it was only a passing shadow from the past. Oh, yes, there is something else, I never asked Merry why she kicked me out and she never explained. Well, for me it was a matter of upmost dignity not to ask why; it would have been a demeaning question to ask, and the answer would have been completely irrelevant!

* * *

Time to take stock

What had I done in the thirteen years since arriving in Britain, except for helping Ben's education (and this wasn't very much)? OK, I'd done my bit for The TransManche Link; producing the Operating Plan for one of the greatest civil engineering projects in the world was something to be proud of but there were others out there who have done similar or perhaps even better than me. In those thirteen years I'd made a reasonable amount of money; I'd copied and mimicked everything around me in Chelsea as much as I could, everything from decent and polite behaviour to elegant clothes and some (still improving) wit! And a great deal more besides, but nowhere near what I was really capable of. I'd made a lot of money, but that money was flowing away from me fast, and I had enjoyed the best food and wine on a daily basis. So what? Big deal. Any illiterate lottery winner could have done better than me; what a waste of time my life had been at that point. In a way, Merry had done me the greatest favour of my life, she had set me free, with real freedom and wings big enough for my first 'trial flight test'. I determined to start not necessarily a new life, (I preferred to continue the same comfortable life in Chelsea of course), but one with freedoms and no obligations or commitments of any sort and with every chance of success. There was, of course, that little matter of success – but in what and how?

Being the vain creature I am, it would, of course, have to be something not even dreamt of before. The next step in mankind's development would have to be something akin to the discovery of fire; the present day crawling with a discovery here, an innovation there, would not do for me. Mankind is still stuck in these particles, electro–magnetism and nuclear power that have had their day.

I don't need fame, I've got brain, was my latest slogan! My achievements would have to be so great and applied in a strictly altruistic manner for all that is British and for the British civilisation only. What a warming thought, the marvellous blending of my scientific dreams combined with the satisfaction of achievement for all to see. My modest thank you for the great British nation, that was all. Of course, I would never demand any reward, I had all the reward I needed, and being British was (and still is) good enough.

I'd been granted British Citizenship in May, 1984; I had the Certificate of Naturalisation No. 1054743 issued by the Home Office and signed by the Assistant Secretary no less. I had to earn my British Citizenship and I am very proud of it too; extremely proud, although I'd done nothing really special, at the time. I'd just applied through Isaacs & Co solicitors and someone had come from the Home Office to talk to me and Merry, and he was very helpful. The 'chap' from the Home Office declared himself satisfied and someone higher up decided that I was good enough to be a naturalised British citizen and that was that!

I went to Mr Isaacs's offices in the City (very luxurious and very much like those of a Gentleman's club in Pall Mall, only smaller!), to take my oath of allegiance to Her Majesty The Queen and all her descendants. I took the swearing allegiance ceremony very seriously and found it somewhat emotional. I'd never sworn allegiance to anybody before and to my surprise Mr Isaacs, who must have attended lots such ceremonies, also became emotional and wiped a tear. Later I found out that his parents had been Jewish refugees who had escaped Nazi Germany. He obviously understood very well what it meant to be a refugee, although he'd never made any conversation or comments about it at any of Merry's parties and frankly, I'd never associated him with deep emotional outbursts. How strange but easy to understand if you have the required life experience.

That bit of yellowish paper with the Government crest and official stamp, the one stating that I was British was the spur to go to great and bigger things. I thought: I *shall* pay back the generous British system and people through my discoveries and inventions and I shall *always* do it for the greatness of this marvellous country I felt I fully belonged to now.

Whenever I meet a new person, eventually I always happen to mention, in passing of course, with a touch of typically British self-deprecation, *you know I am British, really*. And if anybody should insist "Yes, of course you are British, I could see that but where are you from originally?" I have a well prepared answer ready:

"Oh, Chelsea, actually," I casually reply, with a 'modest' smile and a self-assured 'poise'.

And to crown it all, on becoming British I was congratulated by everybody. Merry of course threw an elegant party with the banner **Welcome to us Michael**, very moving indeed. Even Merry's mother managed an open smile and produced a card and a little present for me, the only time she ever did that. Among all the celebrations for my British conversion I got one of the best compliments ever; Mr Isaacs toasted me with the words: "Well done Michael, we could do with some more like you." High praise indeed; I shall proudly bear it in mind till the day I die.

But enough about the past! The new, improved, more determined and more powerful Michael had arrived – with a great deal more to show for himself and even more to come!

New and greater things were waiting for me in my new world of inventions and discoveries. There would be so many changes and that would be for starters only. As for the main 'event' I still had to think what that was going to be but it would be something to change the course of mankind no doubt. Meanwhile I was going to take any idea as it came along, play with it, toy with it, put some effort into it, let it grow, give it wings and carefully, very carefully change the dream into reality. It was that simple and it worked. I swear it was true! There I was, Michael, the unusual, in full flow. You just had to watch me and wonder!

Life – let's invent!

After several false starts, and more unpleasantness from the person whose name I swore I'd never mention again, I settled into a small flat near Sloane Square; I wasn't going to leave Chelsea, under any circumstances! I had the chance of my life for a new, independent beginning, completely on my own and all for myself. I had no longer personal commitments to anybody or anything except to Britain and myself, as part of it. To earn a living I carried on doing temporary consultancy work and every penny I made went straight into my inventions.

It sounds strange, weird even, that a few dozen yards from Sloane Square – the symbol and epitome of Chelsea – there was a guy who's working hard at trying to change the world for the better, instead of enjoying the best that Chelsea had to offer. Being 'free' to admire and 'touch', given the chance, some of the most beautiful creatures that had ever graced this earth had its temptations, of course, and I indulged myself a bit with some success, so much so that I even won the 'regulars' competition (the competition to see who had brought in the most beautiful woman) at The Oriel Brasserie in Sloane square. I won it of course, when I brought in a girl from Georgia – that is Georgia the country from the Caucasian mountains, not the state from USA! – whose name I remember no more. She was really something even by the rarefied heights of Chelsea standards of beauty, and I won the bottle of Cristal champagne which 'the beauty' finished off herself almost alone and then wanted some more! Oh dear!

Then there was Angie, with a body that engendered in most men of all ages that mad, instinctive desire of trying to touch her; enough to say that on a trip to Rome, she had her bum pinched dozens of time by the locals who thought that on seeing a walking statuesque body it was their God given right to molest it. Angie's body was really so attractive to the sex-obsessed Italians that we could not walk 'normally' on the streets of the Eternal City (that is 'normal' as in English; Italians don't seem to have a word for 'normal behaviour' in my experience, but there we are!). When she complained to a 'carabineer' about being pinched and pointed at, the carabineer, fully kitted out with a machine gun and some real cool sunglasses (although it was raining), tried to embrace her, declaring loudly for everyone to hear "But you are a *bella donna*. You make people happy! Let me kiss you!" and he actually tried to kiss Angie on the lips, reinforcing my strong belief that Italian men are the most lecherous in the world! And that in the centre of Rome. I wondered how things must be in the remote parts of Italy! No wonder they needed the Mafia to protect women, as the hotel manager explained to us when he joined us at the bar, uninvited. In fairness he didn't touch Angie with his hands but the eyes could have eaten someone every five seconds or so, he had them!

Angie had many more qualities besides her body and looks and I was seriously considering asking her to come and live with me, for the time being at least. My future inventions would have to wait a bit, Angie was such a perfect woman and she really enjoyed making love to me. I could only see beautiful things in Angie, although she used to spend an inordinate amount of time in the bathroom. I suspected nothing, that is, until the day I saw her kissing deeply on the lips a character who could only be described as a *tramp*. I confronted her. She readily admitted the kiss but the guy was not her lover, he was her drug dealer and the kiss was in fact transferring a drug pill from him to her! This finished our relationship stone dead, then and there.

I could not afford to get involved with anything that would affect my brain and I knew enough biochemistry to understand the dangers of even the most innocuous drugs. Drugs for me were and are a no-no, no to the power of a million – never! Might as well part from Angie, she was a distraction. True, a very attractive distraction. (Why are most distractions in life so attractive? I keep wondering, but no answers are ever forthcoming!)

I worked out a rule of some sort for myself – when uneasy and unwell, if uncomfortable in your own skin, then fall back on discipline. Make easy rules to follow daily, little routines. Have a cappuccino first thing in the morning for instance. In my case, it helps to say a little prayer in the morning as well, but God, it is so hard to pray sometimes – the words do not come in the right way, the thoughts are all over the place, but pray you must!

But still the great inspiration was nowhere to be seen and I was drudging away from one contract to another short time contract, wasting time and burning money!

There were of course other parties interested in me, some of them young and beautiful, some beautiful and not so young, but there was only one left who passed my ultimate test in being 'the right' person. With the experience I'd gained up to that point I developed a little test that proved to be nothing short of brilliant. It went a bit like this, after a few dates with a woman, the next time she'd phone I'd pretend in a horrified voice "Oh darling, I have terrible news, my accountant has disappeared with all my money. I don't know what I'm going to do now!" Nine times out of ten, the phone line went dead, usually to my great relief. There was only one person who asked how she could help. Her name was Margaret and she was 'the one'.

A little bit of sincere kindness means more than all the love stories put together, I thought and I was not wrong, that time I was not wrong! With her meagre resources, Margaret was bringing up three children and had all sorts of problems with a lazy husband but somehow she found the time, the effort, the goodwill and kindness to keep me going. Thank you Margaret!

* * *

Something drastic had to be done. Inspiration, where are you? I kept begging, at times I almost cried in despair, truly pathetic. Despite the clothes, the looks, the pretence, in reality I was slowly becoming the thing I was trying to avoid at all costs – an absolute pretentious wreck with no sense or direction. You should only drink to celebrate an achievement and not drink yourself to a stupor dreaming about success with nothing to show for it! Searching for an answer I remembered an old proverb from the country where I was born. It says, a hungry wolf runs faster and I followed it to almost physical destruction. I cut my intake of calories to fewer than one thousand a day; I stopped drinking alcohol in one fell swoop and after one week of black fasting I began to have moments when I almost collapsed on the street during my long walks on Chelsea Embankment. However, the glorious views and the good weather kept up my spirits somehow and after two weeks or so I was somewhat regenerated, if not bodily, definitely mentally. For me inventing is the supreme form of human intelligence spurred by some sort of rebellion, essential not only to my personal life but eventually for the survival of the human race.

I started seeing things in my instinctive manner and my first invention was inspired from looking at impressive street graphics of a Porsche super car – its brakes more precisely. What a silly thing, I thought, to use friction in trying to stop a wheel, surely there must a more intelligent way of doing it? Let me think about it!

How do you become an inventor? you may ask.

You don't, you are born with the talent for it, very few are so endowed. You are or you are not, and that is true of most of mankind! It is like being a composer (preferably one like Mozart) or a phenomenally skilled football player (preferably one like Messi). Otherwise don't waste your time. And you need a well embedded seed of doubt about almost everything that surrounds you. Question it, however 'normal' it might look. Could it be replaced by something better? Question it, doubt it, and bring up an improved replacement, or even better, something absolutely new. However barmy it might sound today, it could be the normal thing tomorrow. In fact society, by developing a teaching system based on regurgitating old ideas, in a funny way actually makes it easier for new ideas to appear. For a talented inventor that is the easy part, then the main difficulties start. Most people at large couldn't care less about sophisticated inventions as such, and those who care usually do one of two things, they either spit on your new ideas or they nick your ideas and make a fortune in the process (here I speak from my own experience)!

As for the process of inventing in itself, I find it extremely easy and here are the magic steps of inventing, as defined by the great inventors and philosophers of the 19th century:

1. Dream it
2. Visualise it
3. Perfect it
4. Build it

I stared again at the impressive Porsche at its gleaming brakes and I thought *this will be a doddle*.

I started modestly, an inertia braking system: designed to replace the braking system based on friction to a braking system based on inertia, a rather complex mechanical device. To my surprise it actually worked but as is the case with most inventions there was the curse of it working 'too well'. When the device was tested by a Formula One team, the net result was that 'my' braking system had worked so well, that it developed braking forces of G9 when cornering which almost killed the unfortunate test driver and the tyres were shredded at the end of only one lap.

Oh well, I thought, at least I have a British patent granted by the British Patent Office. For the record, patent number GB2350589 with the title 'Inertia Induced Braking System'. I was extremely proud to have had a patent granted from the same office that has granted patents to some of the greatest British inventors and discoverers mankind has ever known, the feeling was at times overwhelming, better than any aphrodisiac, a supreme form of kindness! Frankly, I couldn't care less that the patent could not be put to use to make me a respectable fortune (that a fortune can be respectable is a moot point anyway!); it had already given me much more than that. I am part of this club of British inventors, I belong here, I am integrated, I am British, for real; I know it, I feel it, I live it! Brilliant! I was born in *Oversylvania* but Britain made me. Beat that if you can whoever doubts me (especially me at times!).

It was clear that my patent would not have daily applications until new materials had been developed; as one of my former professors at The Imperial would say, "Give me the materials and I will build anything". Frankly, I was not bothered to go knocking at doors, trying to commercialise my invention, not at that time anyway. Of course, this turned out to be an error of judgement. In my enthusiasm I had forgotten to protect my patent and to my disbelief and chagrin I later discovered that the system I had invented was being used by a big, not so friendly country in the East in the guidance of their intercontinental missiles; in essence, making their ballistic missiles fly along an unpredictable trajectory which made them very hard to intercept, if at all. I should have known straight away that there were certain ways of protecting your invention from being 'appropriated' by a very powerful country or industrial conglomerate.

For my next invention, something in electronics, I made an even bigger mistake. Before even applying for a patent I contacted one of the big Japanese electronics companies with my ideas and explained to them in detail (big, *big* mistake!). We both signed a non-disclosure agreement and I was looking forward to a full and productive cooperation; that was until the Japanese company sent me a letter informing me that they were not interested any longer in cooperating in any future development of my system. As it happened, one of their company employees had had the same idea and knowledge as me. There was an article in the small print of 'the non-disclosure agreement' which stipulated that in this case the company would be fully entitled to the invention. And that was that! Yet another lesson had been learned and when I mentioned it to Ron, there was little sympathy from him. Ron told me straight

"I never thought you were so naïve, Michael. You tell the people of big multinationals about inventions that could make them billions without any legal protection and you expect them not to take advantage? Are you for real?"

I thought Ron's comments hurtful and expected him to show me some understanding, give me some good advice on how to deal with all those sharks, but there was no other word of support for my naïvety!

"Really Michael, what you are doing is ridiculous, might as well go and offer to work for them for no reward whatsoever, no salary or any money at all. Don't you realise that most multinationals are the legalised highway robbers of past times and they behave accordingly – that is the nature of the beast! And before you start lecturing me, just look at how many people they employ!"

Taking into account that Ron was the Vice President of one the top one hundred companies in FT index, a conglomerate producing everything from margarine to top brand perfumes, I took his words very seriously.

"And by the way, Michael, whatever you do, please don't invent a new toothbrush," Ron added smiling. "It looks to me that every single inventor in the world wakes up in the morning, brushes his teeth and thinks 'Eureka' I think I could design / invent a better toothbrush. Yep, the innocuous toothbrush is the most invented item in the world, bar none; believe you me, and most of them come my way!"

I hastened to reassure Ron that inventing new toothbrushes was somehow beyond my 'intellectual dignity'. One day I would invent something so big that it would solve the biggest problem mankind was facing at the moment – the ever increasing thirst for energy. I didn't know at that time what it would be, I would dream it one day, pretty soon, then I would visualise it followed shortly by perfecting it and followed finally by actually producing the working prototype! Meanwhile, I couldn't stop thinking I'd been let down by the whole world and nobody had a kind word for me. Even bloody Ron; I expected a bit more help, a more sympathetic ear, but no chance. We then went to play our weekly tennis session and I gave him a good thrashing which made me feel much better and almost fully relaxed.

"Don't worry Ron, you'll win next time, no doubt about it, you've just had a bad day, you are a good player," I consoled him in true British style – I could play him at this particular game too!

(I've told you, I am much more British than my Certificate of Naturalisation (No. 1054743, Issued by the Home Office, London) could ever prove!

With or without Ron's encouragement, I just carried on inventing, sometimes to amuse myself, sometimes because I could do it! Once, when I read that Mozart (best proof that God really exists!), composed three symphonies and a couple of piano concertos and a few bits and pieces in the space of only three months I decided I should come up with three inventions within three months – and so I did. The first two were so and so, by my standards, an 'intelligent' toaster that would never burn the toast, believe it or not, and the other one was a pre-programmed container to open only in extremely precise locations which was sort of OK but not ground-breaking. However, the third invention was really something completely different, so much so that the Comptroller General of patents telephoned me personally to congratulate me pointing out that he had never encountered such a remarkably unique and original invention. Without going into too many details, this invention formally called 'Synchronised Remote Action System' (Patent No. GB2421157) did away with passwords of any sort for computers or any communication between computers, and practically made the need for encryption irrelevant – any encryption however good, whoever the author is, human or machine, will be broken eventually, the Germans found this out to their cost during WW2 and all companies and most individuals find it out to their cost almost every day. Whatever lock is made by a human it will be un-locked by a human, as the proverb goes in dear old *Oversylvania*!

How do you as a human invent something that can not be undone by another human?

I had the answer. Simply bring in an external element that no human being or machine could affect in the least, the thing that flows unabated or un-affected by any obstacle or events, the unique 'constant' uniquely available not only on earth but in the universe itself. If I could only define this unique constant, available in its unique form for every user, I'd be well on my way to a really sensational invention.

I spent many weeks mulling over this particular, mysterious constant, until one day, during one of my favourite walks in Royal Hospital Road and on the Thames Embankment, I did finally find this mysterious and elusive constant so badly needed for my new invention. I did say *Eureka!*, sort of, but I did not jump into the Thames, much too muddy anyway and at low tide, however great my discovery! The answer, like most answers to the most troublesome questions, was a simple one and readily available for all to see. I instantly realised that what we call *time*, the measuring of the movement of the planets, was the constant I needed; nobody could modify or affect in the least the movement of the planets, or to put it another way, my X-factor constant would remain a constant until someone somehow could make the earth rotate backwards or take a walk towards a different galaxy. Gravity would see that this would never happen; there was no chance of something like that any time soon, if ever. Should it happen most people would be dead, killed by the weather cataclysm that would follow and the rest would have bigger problems to survive than to take any notice of new discoveries!

In practical but very broad terms, for certain reasons it meant that by introducing the factor *time* into any communication between computers, the speed of communication between the computers (in my case it was one hundredth of a one millionth of a second on my prototypes fitted with a miniaturised atomic clock) made interception impossible – and nobody could write a password or anything else so fast; goodbye hacking in cyber space! In practical terms the connected computers within a network would exchange time recognition patterns (sort of passwords), self-devised by the computer itself and nobody would know what the next pass-pattern based on the flow of time would be – not even the owner of the network. Of course, that meant also goodbye to passwords of any sort, face recognition, fingerprints and all sorts of what I consider Mickey Mouse solutions just waiting to be broken by any eleven-year-old, early morning in his bed with his laptop on the pillow, just for fun!

I built a prototype which left me almost penniless and I had to do all sorts of menial jobs by my standards, but very well paid jobs, mainly abroad to raise money. I became an economic migrant to other countries, temporarily at least, but everything was worth pursuing; this invention was really something special. Too special, unfortunately, as it turned out later. Of course, this time I was careful to put some false trails in my patent description publicly available, as an extra guarantee that this time nobody would steal my patent with whatever subterfuge or simply by just ignoring me – it would have been clear to anyone that I could not possibly fight a big corporation or even a State in any court of law.

In fairness, there was a great deal of interest to start with, which pleased me no end. The fact that I came with something that nobody had ever thought of before gave me the greatest pleasure. The fact that I'd become financially secure again was not to be ignored either. I went to talk about my invention to the huge companies responsible for most IT technology and its applications, but soon I discovered a curious pattern in everybody's behaviour. Everyone would show a real keen interest to start with, and all would go smoothly until they asked

"How could we break into the system if we needed to?"

The answer was pretty simple

"You can't! Not unless you can make time run backwards, the solar system would need serious adjustment if that were to happen and I cannot see it happening anytime soon," I would heartily joke. But with time my joke fell flat and somehow after high initial interest I'd never hear from the interested parties again. It took me years to understand why everybody would suddenly lose interest in a system proven to stop any form of hacking, while at the same time bleating about all their measures of security that wouldn't stop a dedicated hacker playing havoc with to his heart's content.

Then one day, a Mr Snowden, a CIA contractor, defected to Russia with billions of encrypted data for Russians to amuse themselves with and for me to understand why all those big companies had not wanted a system that could not be broken into. According to Mr Snowdon's undisputed evidence, having a system that the information services could not access or rather, intercept any data, was a big NO, the very reddest of red lines to cross. The fact that my system was self-generating access codes that lasted for connection of only a fraction of a millionth of a second was not the anti-hacking solution they were looking for, if 'solution' is the right word. Most of the interception work done by any information agency would have been undone by the impossibility of 'hacking in' friends or foes alike; some of Mr Snowden's revelations were actually funny if not scary – CIA agents in Berlin spying and hacking into Mrs Merkel's phone were the butt of most comedians, but the fact that the Americans did not trust the Germans seventy years after the second world war, was altogether less funny.

Oh well, I had to sigh and resign – that was the nature of the beast and I was not in a position to challenge it even if I'd felt like it. Still, like with most happenings in my life there is something to smile about when I recall my efforts to promote a brilliant 'problem saving system' and nobody concerned being in the least bit interested despite letting themselves be exposed to the army of hackers all over the world with lots of time on their hands and a fair dose of criminal intent! (You see, my English improved as well during this process!)

Among the institutions I approached with my foolproof cyber defence invention were a few banks in the City; I did not approach any of the Big Four, as my experience taught me, they never replied to such things like improved technology if it did not originate from 'their own clients'! I did, however, approach several smaller, private banks and one of them, a very old and reputable bank in the City and Europe, always a 'family affair', replied in a friendly manner and I was to be seen by one of its vice presidents no less. I went to see this particular gentleman whom I knew was also a member of The Royal Academy of Science – a most unusual occurrence as banking, in my opinion at least, has more to do with 'sleight of hand' than a 'creative mind' (not including creative accounting, a bank's prerogative, of course!). I took a taxi to this particular bank with its grand offices in the City and was received in a polite and pleasant manner straightaway, most unusual compared to all my other experiences in other places. The bank's Vice-President, an elderly gentleman with features and manner of speaking that sent me back to Edwardian Times, received me warmly too and straight away asked me:

"How did you get here, did you find it hard to get to this place?"

"Oh no," I reassured him, "I took a taxi."

"Oh, you did," was his reply while, coincidentally of course, showing me his Public Transport Pass. OK, point taken I thought, rather embarrassed with myself.

"You see Michael, can I call you Michael?" and without waiting for my approval he continued "I must say I am fascinated by your invention – really impressive, how did you come by it?"

I was only too happy. If there is anything I like talking about more than myself, it's my inventions. I explained to the gentleman in detail how I'd gone about it, the thinking process, and I made it sound much simpler and easier that the realities of it, but altogether I was happy with my presentation.

"Fascinating," he said, "truly fascinating. I must congratulate you on your invention and all your endeavours. This is remarkable, truly remarkable. Unfortunately, I must disappoint you but we are unable to use your system; we talked about it a great deal within these four walls and I tell you why. The system as I understand it does not require a password that you memorise and all that sort of thing. Am I correct in assuming that?"

"Yes, of course you are, it is the actual computer independent of me or anybody else which does the synchronisation as I call it."

"Well, you see, *that* is the insurmountable problem, Michael. Forget your scientific hat for a second and imagine you are a simple customer of the bank. All a bank's customer cares about is the safety of his money, deposits and the like – he or she will grumble about the bank, the services provided and so on, but what a customer cares most about is the safety of his or her deposits.

"Now imagine that I told my customers with a serious face and in writing, that as from tomorrow they would no longer need a password to access their accounts! I tell you what would happen, they would queue around the block to remove their deposits and by lunchtime this bank would be bankrupt for the first time in five hundred years. Of course, you realise I could not take this very probable risk, however impressed I am by your invention. I wish you all the best and when you make your fortune remember that we are an extremely reliable bank!"

I left wondering that should I ever make any serious money I'd return to that bank to buy it, just to amuse myself!

* * *

There is a refuge that I still cherish most, Kensington Gardens, and this was the place where one morning I first thought about the *Energy of Time* or VERA as I first called it (Vera being the name of my mother, I just couldn't think of a better name). During the previous night I'd had, seriously, a very strange dream. I was covered in a multitude of colourful spheres that were growing and shrinking; and engulfing one another in a smooth flow, it was like those Russian dolls that the moment you open there is another smaller one inside, only in this case the small ones were engulfing the bigger ones in a continuous flow overwhelming everything. Those little colourful balls with their everchanging size were obviously the waves of TIME. The TIME not as a dimension, but TIME as the *energy of time*! It was all so clear and simple, all open for everyone to see. Time as a dimension and relativity and all past time nonsense was just that, nonsense! TIME is not the movement of the planets, it is the energy that moves the planets, spins the earth and everything else, continuously energising the smallest particles and beyond! Of course, how simple, how brilliant and how rewarding everything was!

I had just discovered or invented the new 'fire' to power the world, the new energy that would be the answer and solution to mankind's eternal problem – the need for energy. It all made sense. Gravity holds the universe in place and VERA (Energy of Time) powers the universe. I quickly realised that if I were right, and RIGHT I WAS, this would mean the end of electromagnetism and particles, the shackles of mankind's development, how quaint and clear everything was! I'd discovered the *Energy of Time*, but it was just a theory as the detractors would have it. Most people dismissed it from the start; science journals would have nothing to do with it, even *Nature* a science publication for which I have a great deal of time and respect rejected my papers twice, second time stating clearly that it was 'speculative' and as such couldn't be taken seriously – this brought a smile to my face thinking that the whole capitalist system is speculative in almost its entirety and it seemed to be working! What *Nature* required from me was what is called a peer review (a review, preferably a positive one, from people in the same field). As my discovery was the next step from particle physics and electromagnetism, there was no one else thinking like me – it was, I pointed out, unsuccessfully as it happened, like asking the Wright brothers of aeroplane fame development for a peer review from the captains of sailing ships! No takers!

From all the publications I approached the only one that showed some sympathy and interest was, believe it or not, Financial Times. Although they would not publish my work **VERA – The Energy of Time** at least they were wishing me good luck!

I was made of sterner stuff than that. I am British; I'd do it the British way; I'd fight come what may! I would fight this one, this was non-negotiable; had to fight with all its repercussions.

BBC2 refused even to have me on a scientific debate; their rejection came with some advice along the lines of: make a stir of some sort, try and get people interested and perhaps they could fit me in their schedule sometime in the future; approaching some student debating societies should be worth trying and good luck!

The BBC can be marvellous at times and I've always had a soft spot for it, but this time I'd just ignore their advice! Brilliant! I thought and promptly approached some of the famous student debating societies, with very mixed results.

My former uni had a "very heavy schedule over the next few years", a blatant lie, but I managed to have an informal chat with some of the committee where I explained the *Energy of Time* and how it worked, all generalities mainly. Out of the fourteen people who attended my presentation, thirteen were totally dismissive of it, but one said "I think you might have something here." To my ears the highest praise I ever got and the strongest encouragement ever. Afterwards I approached the Oxford Union and received back a rather insulting letter telling me in no uncertain terms that the Oxford debating society would never be interested in such absurd ideas as my *Energy of Time*. Besides being rude and frankly vulgar in their letter, they were also pompous: *No further correspondence will be entertained* was their final sentence! Twenty years of expensive education to produce this standard reply looked pretty expensive to me. On the other hand, being rejected by the Oxford Debating Society turned out to be a badge of honour; they had form! They had recently been banning anyone whose family had not been 'politically correct' for the last seven generations or so!

Still, I was more convinced of my *Energy of Time* than ever and the refusal of a society busy re-writing history would not put me off. I got a much friendlier response from the Cambridge Union, which was to be expected, obviously; I should have thought of them to start with, stuff the Oxford lot! Cambridge was obviously miles ahead of Oxford in debating new scientific discoveries. After all, some of the greatest inventions for mankind have been made at Cambridge: the DNA discovery, to give just one example! Oxford is just a 'talking shop' when all is said and done! Are they not the debating society that in the 1930s voted against having a war with Nazi Germany? That tells you all you need to know! And Cambridge is the classier too. Easy to spot the difference!

The Chairman of the Cambridge Union sent me a very sympathetic letter and after admitting that he knew little of the scientific matter I was bringing to the Union for debate, he thought it was new and exciting and so why not? I was invited to give my presentation, modestly entitled **The Energy of Time – the supreme form of Energy** and to my deepest satisfaction a date and time was established. I prepared myself, I rehearsed in front of the mirror and for a few seconds I even contemplated doing something about my accent but I thought I'd sound like a phoney and that perhaps it was not the place or the time for such things.

The day of my communicating to the some of the brightest minds in the world was nearing fast and everything was ready when I received an unexpected call from the Cambridge Union organiser, who informed me in a very apologetic manner that there had been a dreadful mistake. There had been a double booking, sort of, and someone else had actually booked first on the date and at the time of my presentation. He was embarrassingly apologetic, I almost felt sorry for the guy and told him I understood. He assured me that a new date and time would be found for me and they would be in touch. OK, I told myself, things happen, and I was pretty relaxed about this small hiccup with the Cambridge Union booking system. I was a great deal less understanding when I discovered who had been given priority by the Society: *Madame Sin* from Streatham. A former Madame who kept a high class brothel for the great and good was the esteemed society's first choice!

But life or rather the *Energy of Time* marches on implacably and was there at the vanguard of it. I have spent years and years, about ten of them, trying to explain to everybody with half a minute to listen, that the time for electromagnetism and particles and all these things we take for granted is running out, that there is a better world waiting for all of us, everyone on earth, in their lifetime; a world beyond electromagnetism and fancy particles – none of it would exist without the *Energy of Time*. I developed it further, explaining new things every time, going deeper in detail but to little effect.

I published at my own expense a little brochure entitled rather grandly **Thus Rule I, The Energy of Time** that I couldn't give away, never mind try to sell. To amuse myself, whenever I did get the chance, I'd give one away and write a dedication on the lines of *If you understand this, you are much more intelligent than I'll ever be.*

It raised a smile or two!

Of course, I got more correct every time, ever so satisfying, but after ten years of effort I had nothing to show for it in real terms, as Ron pointed out to me in his rather unmerciful way. It was hurtful, even worse, he was right. I could preach till I was blue in the face, few had time or pretended to find the very time to listen to me, and even when they did, this was more out of politeness than anything else. Well, it *is* British politeness and in a certain manner it helped and I'm sure they meant it, for a second or two! A quantum of solace perhaps, but it helped; it was an implicit sign of support for the barmiest theory they'd ever heard – but it helped.

My thoughts went ever further ahead in the world of the mysterious *Energy of Time* that everybody was ignoring. The very latest discoveries in astrophysics proved my theory and were yet another nail in the coffin of the 'marvellous world of electromagnetism and particles. In 1993 I had already predicted the existence of dark matter or dark energy and I was laughed out of court – at this point it turned out that this 'dark' thingy made up almost eighty per cent of the universe; at the same time I was predicting that the galaxies were actually accelerating and it was clear to see that they were moving faster than the speed of light, otherwise we wouldn't have noticed their accelerating speed given the distance. Two guys were awarded the Nobel Prize ten years later for something similar, good luck to them! I had bigger fish to fry and fry I would!

Integrating, final

I'd been doing this induction 'thingy' for a few years by this point, I had more time and more interest in what happened around me now that I had broken free from Merry (was 'kicked out' was closer to the truth, but I won't dwell on the past). In an extraordinary way, being asked to go it on my own made me into some sort of internal refugee once again, a totally unexpected and really earth-shattering experience. OK, I was already well established in Britain, I was more integrated than any new refugee; I was financially secure, but still I could easily have described myself as being down and out! To compensate somehow, I became more involved with my induction routine which gave me a great deal of solace and reminded me continuously that there were much bigger dramas and at times, tragedies being 'played for real' all around me. Bigger things than my personal problems were at play and the elections of 1997 brought what I thought would be if not heaven on earth something pretty close to it, at least! A new Labour government, with a charismatic leader and a huge majority had just won the elections under the slogan *Things can only get better*! Didn't they just! I must admit being swept away by the enthusiasm for change, and faithful to my democratic principle of always voting for the opposition, I voted for Labour and Tony just for change's sake!

Tony Blair, "just call me Tony", was on an unstoppable charm offensive and everyone seemed to like this 'honest' politician; what a refreshing change after all those 'nasty Tories'! He was so popular than even the Tory establishment seemed to like him, those who plotted and got rid of Mrs Thatcher seemed to be pleased as well, except for the Richard (remember him, the one who stabbed her in the back?). He didn't like Tony one little bit and was purported to have described Tony's eyes as "the eyes of evil", very strong stuff by the British standards of electioneering and how right Richard turned out to be, perhaps for the first time in his political life, but at that time nobody would listen to him! In the years to come hundreds of thousands of dead Iraqi civilians and tens of millions of refugees, all victims of Tony's lies and manipulations would have vouched for Tony's evil. But all those victims and the wars were far in the future and Britain or 'New Britain' – freshly renamed to rhyme with New Labour – was enjoying a sustained period of prosperity. The net result was that the Labour Party's chief ideologue, some sort of Prince of Darkness who kept resigning for being found out for committing 'small transgressions' with his mortgage and the like, would cheerfully declare he was very comfortable with rich people, or something similar. In the years to follow, Tony and most of his 'lieutenants' would become very rich, multi-multi-millionaires, just by chance and luck (but I don't believe it).

Among the many promises made by the New Labour government was something about the refugees and a 'multi-cultural society', which I must admit pleased me initially. I didn't stand to benefit materially from the change in policy and I assumed that any change would be better for those who needed it most, the refugees. I couldn't have been more wrong when I dismissed their ideas of a multi-cultural society as some sort of electoral spin (New Labour turned out to be the super-masters of spin, unless you didn't put a spin on whatever, don't bother was their slogan and belief!). But this newly created word and philosophy was to have disastrous results for the very structure of British society and stood against everything in my experience of working with refugees. Gone was the idea of integration and in came the dogma of multiculturalism with the net result of creating religious, cultural, political and ethnic ghettos. For me, this was the end of my involvement with working for refugees.

Soon after the election of 1997, when I was doing my 'induction' for a group of five middle eastern refugees, two people from the council came to witness unannounced the process of induction in full flow. It only took the visitors ten minutes or so before they intervened and asked me to come and talk to them in one of the council's offices. They introduced themselves as being the Head and the Deputy Head of a newly formed 'Multicultural Integration Department' within the council.

"What do you think you are doing Michael?" was their first rather aggressive question.

"Well, I'm trying to help and I think it works, we manage to achieve quite a lot," I replied.

"Don't you realise what you are doing? To put it simply to you, we think you are brainwashing these people and we have had complaints about it."

"There was no coercion of any sort; they just came because they wanted to hear how their life here could be made easier, more comfortable. Believe you me, I went through this, I know from my own experience how much effort is required to try and integrate within the community or society when you are a refugee with hardly any knowledge about your new surroundings. To give you an example I don't tell them how to dress, I tell them what a laundrette is for and how to use it. That is all, hardly brainwashing!"

I was getting uneasy and I am not at my best when on the defensive.

"I deal with the practicalities of living and you are coming with slogans which are meaningless and damaging. Look, Britain is an island, a platform in the North Sea if you want a comparison. I am just helping with their induction on this North Sea platform. Your multiculturalism will end up nothing short of a disaster, one culture plus another culture makes two cultures, not one better culture as you seem to believe. Diversifying will weaken the country and the way I know the British people, the 'natives' if you like, they will not put up with it for long."

It turned out to be prophetic words just shouted by me in anger, but the Brexit Referendum twenty years later would prove how most British people felt; in essence they rejected certain essential forms of a 'multicultural society' to the dismay of the 'Elite' or 'Establishment' which Canute style, ignored the realities of life outside Westminster, The Royal Borough of Kensington and Chelsea and, of course, the rather well to do champagne socialist parts of Islington!

"You are obviously not only missing the point but your attitude contradicts all that a multicultural society stands for and that is the aim of the government now," the multicultural duo replied.

"We have many studies by experts who prove that the best way for refugees is not to integrate as you insist, but to cherish their own values and culture. We are now a multicultural society, and we are not Nazis to tell everyone what they must do and must not do so that everybody in society is the same. What we must do is to encourage the refugees to be themselves, to keep and expand their beautiful customs and habits; it will enrich this country's culture and civilisation!"

There was no way I was going to accept this sort of reasoning and promptly replied

"Look, all I'm trying to do is to make their life easier. Frankly, I fail to see how the multicultural society as you call it, helps him or her to find and enrol with a GP, or where to shop so he can manage to survive on the meagre support from the Government until they can find a proper job. There are all sorts of small things to be done to fulfil the bureaucratic requirements of day to day living; they need help with translations and the like, and that is what I do, all on *my* time and money, it costs the council nothing."

I reasoned in vain. It was a waste of time arguing with halitosis, and that was the way I felt; depressed and rejected. I was in vain. The 'multicultural duo' had their own, well-rehearsed arguments and facts.

"We could manage what you are doing now in a proper, well researched manner. You may not be aware that the council has published a comprehensive guide for all new and old refugees in ninety-three different languages and here it is," and they produced a big volume A4 size of about two hundred pages. "It covers all the refugees need to know in every single language spoken in our borough; it tells them in their own language about almost everything they need to make themselves at home," the duo concluded in a rather triumphal manner.

I quickly scanned through the impressive publication, embellished with photographs of smiling refugees dressed in a way I had never encountered one, of all skin colours except white (the majority of political refugees at the time were white actually!) and to my amazement I promptly observed a big oversight in the publication.

"You said there are ninety-three languages in here?" I smiled, pointing to the volume.

"Yes, every single language spoken in our borough," they both confirmed.

"Is there nobody speaking English in this borough anymore?" I gently enquired. "I see not a word of English, not even one in the whole volume. Not even the council's name, for Pete's sake!

The duo recovered quickly:

"The refugees don't need it in English; they have it in their own language, so they can preserve their own language and customs, this is what multiculturalism is all about!" came their triumphal conclusion.

"Yes, but the people around them, the 'natives', they all speak English. How will the refugees integrate with the 'natives'?" I queried.

The duo was ecstatic.

"You prove our point without even realising it. The refugees will have their own community; they will preserve their customs, their religion and everything else they come with and we'll all learn a great deal from them; we must be grateful to them and the state will have to pay for it and we'll take care of it."

"Yes," I conceded, "this is all nice and definitely helpful, but your volume of 'help and advice' is just words, while what I do is to provide a little help with the daily physical chores, that's all."

"Oh no," they both heartily disagreed. "What *you* are doing is trying to brainwash them; you tell them all that nonsense about Magna Carta, and feudal laws, and how great the British Empire was, and British achievements and the like—"

"This is true, at times when some of the refugees are depressed, homesick and the like, I'll do my best to cheer them up by giving examples of previous refugees who went on to become great achievers in the field of science, business, politics, you name it – you'll find it has happened in Britain. As for the desire of most of the political refugees to eventually go back to their own country and become active in politics without fearing for their lives, there are dozens, if not hundreds of examples – anyone from Lenin to Ho Chi Minh have spent time as refugees in London, freely espousing their political creeds with extraordinary results and consequences. Many present-day political leaders all over the world have spent time as political refugees in Britain, some doing the most menial jobs to survive in an extravagantly expensive London, but firm in their beliefs and aims. There is nothing extraordinary, it doesn't even make the newspapers, that some former political refugee who once worked as a security guard at IKEA is now the democratically elected President of an important African country, and very proud of it. One of the things I like to do when walking in London with a small gathering of political refugees is to point out the many blue plaques with foreign sounding names, commemorating the achievements by so many former refugees to Britain in so many different fields. Seeing the statue of Gandhi or Mandela always goes down a treat! My favourite one is 'that chap', Marconi was his name, the one who invented 'the radio' and happened to be an immigrant to British shores. I always mention Marconi but I skip the little detail that when he came to British shores the reception from the authorities was not what he'd expected. Fearing that this Italian 'gentleman' might be a terrorist who'd brought with him this prototype of what he called 'a radio' – nobody having heard of such a contraption before, it could therefore easily be a bomb! As a result the customs officers promptly destroyed the radio prototype to Marconi's chagrin and despair. Still this did not stop him from achieving all his aims, and radio was invented and demonstrated in Britain through sheer work and determination!"

"Ah," the duo intervened, "this is another thing about you, you're trying to brainwash and indoctrinate the refugees with false and misleading descriptions of The British Empire and its evil works. You never mention the slave trade, you never tell them how much Britain has exploited their countries to make London a rich place and so on and so on."

I made one last effort.

"Look, as I keep telling you, I only provide a little physical help with their daily needs. I might at times tell them my personal opinions as a former political refugee myself.'

"We know about you Mr Michael, you live in Chelsea, what do you know about real poverty and suffering? You know nothing!"

This was their poisonous and simply untrue assumption and as far as they were concerned this was the only 'truth' worth having. But there was another truth, a thing I'd never mentioned before to anyone in Britain. I took my shirt off and I showed them a scar on my body, a very long one, the result of one of my kidneys having been removed after being tortured by *Oversylvanian* secret police.

"This is how much I know about being a dissident and being tortured for it, as most of these people have been. This is my bond of knowledge that I have in common with these people irrelevant of their political opinions, creed, race, whatever. But obviously no doubt you have your studies done by someone who 'has heard about torture', spoken to his circle of mates about it no doubt, and 'let's make it some sort of intolerant official policy' – that is what our focus group tells us, no doubt!"

I couldn't help pointing out that charity was not the preserve of the left or right wing; although in my experience it is the right minded who give most to charity, which I find perfectly normal, but not this lot! The conversation with the duo was all downhill from then on. As to be expected the words 'Nazi sympathiser' and 'fascist tendencies' were soon being bandied about, which I found particularly distasteful given the origins of most of my family. I realised at last, for good, that you can never win an argument against halitosis, you'll always lose! It is as simple as that.

I was invited by the newly arrived security guard to leave the council premises immediately. Apparently, I've been banned for life from using its facilities and, this is not a joke, the council will send me a bill for my past use of council premises for my meetings with the refugees.

"I will pay it if is written in the English language only!"

To my bewilderment, there is no other word, I suddenly became a persona non grata just for having helped other people. It took me many weeks to get over my encounter with the new political wing of New Labour. Things had not gone 'my way' in many respects, to put it mildly! The 'liberally minded left' are as vicious and poisonous as the most 'closed minded' right-wingers, there is no doubt about it! They both bring poison to any debate but the right-wingers tend always to be the richer ones and the left-wingers the more vicious ones! Say what you will but this is my experience talking here!

The collapse of the Berlin Wall brought extraordinary changes all over Europe and even further afield. Also the nature of the newly arriving refugees changed almost completely overnight, and by the year 2000, the huge majority of immigrants were strictly economic migrants coming overwhelmingly from Eastern European former communist countries. Most of them were not interested one little bit in politics or human rights and the like; they were interested in only what was in it for them and unashamedly demanded the rights of the refugees, claiming housing and all available social benefits usually reserved for political refugees. The big watershed came in 2004 when Poland and the Balkan countries joined The European Union and the British Government opened the borders to any-one from those countries, estimating that 'at most' there would be around 13 000 immigrants turning up. True to form and in keeping to the custom of producing the most misleading forecast in the history of mankind, the true number of immigrants was just under one million! Even by Whitehall standards of stupid forecasting this was a real big one but the Mandarins just shrugged it off as one of those things! It might have had something to do with the rumour that Tony, that is Tony, the Prime Minister, was comfortable with the extraordinary number of immigrants to Britain as long as they were white and Christian, just a rumour I heard from a neighbour of mine, a senior civil servant working in the Home Office.

The truth is that social events were overtaking me and it was time for pastures new in my life and talents. The infinite fields of inventions were waiting for me and if I was to make a change this was the time. Time to invent something that would change the world for good! That would do nicely for me and everybody else in this marvellous land, temporarily taken over by a criminally minded actor and his sycophantic fans. I was sure it would not last!

* * *

If there is one thing that will help any newcomer to the British shores above all else, it is that of learning the art of satire, smooth sophisticated satire as an answer to any verbal attack; and if that fails, a newcomer should try and apply the art of self-deprecation (a much tougher approach and for which one requires a great deal of self-control), which can hurt much more than any verbal attack.

Think of yourself no longer as a refugee; forget the self-pitying and generally feeling sorry for yourself. Make room, first of all for a bit of gratitude for the people of this country, however strange or perhaps uncaring their attitude may look to you. Perhaps the 'natives' are hard on some of the habits you have grown up with.

Alphabet

There are things we take for granted by forgetting that most of them must have been invented by someone, and I find it very amusing and rewarding to imagine the actual process of inventing or discovering something that will serve all mankind, with all the participant characters in its 'detailed human touch' as I call it.

The most fascinating in its own development must be the alphabet, you know, the thing you use when you text, letters as we call them for those less initiated! Some still think that remembering twenty-one signs (letters for those with a higher education) is a bit over the top – we ought to have an 'app' for it!

About four thousand years ago somewhere in Ancient Babylon, a young scribe, Salik was his name, one sunny day (have you noticed, days were always sunny in Antiquity, give or take a flood or two!) decided to invent a proper alphabet, easy to use, easy to understand, available to everyone. He was fed up with using pictorial symbols known as hieroglyphics where each word had its own symbol; that was extremely limited in its scope and only understood and used by very few people. So, the young man decided to invent the written language and replace the oral tradition with a written one, having little inkling of the impact it would have on civilisation. He must have thought there would be some sort of reward at the end of his toils, even an acknowledgement from the All Mighty Ruler. In any case, if he succeeded, and succeed he would – by any standards he was a very determined individual – then he would be acknowledged as the best scribe ever by all other scribes, and that was all he wanted. Acknowledgement!

First, he noticed that the sounds used by people around him were similar and repetitive, then came the idea that instead of drawing the symbol of an object, he would use symbols for the actual sounds made by people talking about the very object. He took perhaps the easiest word, and the most common one, *mama*, and broke it into two signs, one for 'm' and one for 'a'. Then he took a longer word, pronounced it loudly many times and designed new signs for each sound. He expected there would be hundreds and hundreds of signs, after all, hardly any two people spoke with the same tonality, not to mention the constant swearing and cursing noises, and almost everybody's sound was different. But he wisely combined the visual with the phonetic and to make a long story short, he ended up with twenty-two separate signs which he could successfully combine for almost any word in his native language.

Well, as any inventor worth his salt knows, inventing is easy compared to 'marketing the invention', to use a modern expression! Same happened most likely to our hero. Obviously, nobody was interested in his invention in the least! For a start, there were too many scribes around already and everybody knew that, frankly, the scribes never did any meaningful work, like toiling in the fields for instance, or fighting in the never-ending wars. Fancy bringing yet more writing! For what? Even the Mighty Ruler first decided it was a waste of time and resources, just now when he was preparing to invade Northern Iraq. But Salik pleaded his case, fought for it, tried to persuade everybody that with time the system would work. All in vain and, in despair, Salik decided to write the very popular story of The Flood using his invention, the alphabet. It was done, elegantly written on a clay cylinder (now in the British Museum, where else?), with a myriad of details about Noah's Ark, the way it was built, the materials used, the animals taken, the shape of the boat, the lot. And, a real stroke of genius marketing this one, Salik made it clear in his story that the then present All Mighty Ruler was a direct descendant from Noah and had, obviously, inherited all Noah's extraordinary qualities, and more.

How things can change overnight! The Almighty Ruler was smart and vain enough to appreciate that being praised God-like in this first type of 'social media' was not to be missed. So much so, that he postponed the ritual annual invasion of Northern Iraq and dedicated all efforts to implement this new tool, bound to bring prosperity and happiness to whoever would use it. And everybody would have to use this particular alphabet, under the pain of death. As it happened, the Almighty Ruler was not much into multiculturalism and the like. One language, one alphabet and that was that!

The rest is history, now you know who to blame for 'texting'! But what happened to Salik? After being allowed to kiss the All Mighty's slipper (that was the equivalent of being granted a knighthood in today's currency, not to be sniffed at!), Salik, quite unwisely, decided to go into business, marketing his invention, in partnership with the Phoenician pirates of all people, who promptly sold him as a slave to the Greeks and flogged the copyright for the first alphabet to everyone in sight at half price on special offer.

The Greeks, even smarter, promptly copied the invention and 'invented' their own alphabet, which at the time of writing this story, goes, I think, like this:

I

O

U

And again, and again, and again!

The Moral is: Let's hope nobody invents a stupid I-alphabet! Twitter is bad enough as it is!

Being British

What is being British? Strange as it may sound there is no standard definition of 'Britishness', and that is part of its charm. I think I might have brought an extra little dimension with my particular 'britishness' but British I am and so I shall die!

I am the most British Person I am aware of, and so I shall die! I know, it sounds pretentious but it is sincerely true!

Don't attack your hosts by bitterly complaining about their leaders and everybody's general behaviour, including that of other refugees. It is no good complaining about the weather either, it won't change. You'd be better advised to pray for global warming if you want real change in the weather in this country! If the British are to be taken as an example, the 'natives' can do all the moaning in the world about almost everything much better than anybody else, with more skill and composure and sometimes even in a witty manner and with a multi-colourful vocabulary covering every conceivable type of accent. I've been here many years now; I've achieved quite a bit (I must remember at times to be slightly modest, one doesn't go around boasting about oneself!) but the thing is that I am still miles behind in the Brits' supreme art of moaning; I don't think I've got the talent for it and come what may, I shall always have a soft spot for Britain (well, Chelsea mainly to start with!) that I just could not join the moaning chorus. If I could come up with a witty remark, preferably to a large audience, things would improve, obviously – I am still working on this one. There is always something to amuse me, especially their art of understatement and whenever I need a smile or even a chuckle I remember the last speech of the Chelsea Society President (it goes without saying that I am a member of the Chelsea Society, obviously!); it went a bit like this:

"One of the great events in our Society's calendar this summer was the cricket match against the team of Anglesey Arms, consisting of former professional players while our team was entirely amateurs. Despite this handicap, our team put up a splendid performance, every single player excelled in his duties, the team made us proud and I warmly congratulate them. Of course we lost!"

This extraordinary sort of behaviour, if properly understood is a great lesson in the way most 'natives' approach their life; nothing seems to be too serious to be taken seriously. In dear old *Oversylvania* there is a saying: 'Everything is negotiable except death'! The local version would be something on the lines of 'Everything can be ridiculed, even death'! This is not something easily understood. I remember my horror when a member of the British Royal family, Lord M, was assassinated by the IRA blowing up his boat. Ben, aged ten at the time, cheerfully came home from his Westminster school asking all of us:

"What's in a thousand bits and flying?" And without waiting for a reply he offered his own version "It is Lord M!" Ben triumphantly explained!

Merry and her mother just smiled politely but I was horrified. When I recovered from the shock I asked Ben:

"Where did you get this 'joke' from?"

"Oh, everybody knows it at school, good one isn't it?"

Well, the British sense of humour is something else that seems to be for the exclusive use of the 'natives'. At times I try to chip in with what polite people call "continental humour" with 'polite success' (it helps to smile politely or if in doubt, just ignore it!)

There is something else that I don't think I've encountered in any other country; given my work, I've been in forty-eight countries, worked in eighteen countries, mainly as a highly paid ex-pat consultant (officially) but as a temporary migrant worker all over the world in reality, strictly to make money so I could finance my 'mad ideas' – or brilliant inventions – take your choice! But there is no place that allows a person the amount of privacy and solitude that Britain does; vital requirements for the successful 'lonely' inventor. I have lived in my last flat for over twenty-one years, I know, remotely and vaguely only two of my twenty-four neighbours; I must have spoken to them at the most half a dozen times a year, perhaps I should cut it down a bit, not to become too over-familiar! "It isn't done" as Merry would have said, and let's keep it that way, that's good enough. Everyone minds their own business and as an inventor I like it more than anything. The funny thing is, however, that despite everyone jealously guarding their privacy, the 'natives' love street parties and gathering together occasionally, once a year or so – I told you they are a strange race, what better example do you want?

The 'natives'' passion for privacy goes so far as to refuse to have identity cards (never mind carrying them at all times). Based on Magna Carta (first edition 1216), the bedrock of the present day British legal system, it says nothing about identity cards which is a good excuse for the overwhelming opinion to have nothing of the sort. Even when one of Britain's most popular prime ministers, popular in the sense of being either a charismatic leader or a war criminal (again, take your choice!) tried very hard to introduce an ID system, the project came a cropper, as the 'natives' simply wouldn't stomach it and everybody was horrified at the cost of the project for a start. It sounds extraordinary that in a country obsessed now by the huge influx of migrant workers (not to be confused with the bona fide refugees), no serious politician would mention the prickly subject of ID cards, not even in passing! As for the much admired, former Prime Minister, history is eventually catching up with him and he has already been described, even by his friends, as "toxic" while his enemies, most of the country at the last count, want him dispatched to the Hague to stand trial for alleged war crimes. Meanwhile, he continues to accumulate million after million from all sorts of sources, and, like a former Miss Universe, tries to make a comeback thirty years later after being chemically and surgically enhanced.

Mr Root and being offended

Very early I learned another 'trick' from the 'natives', a vital one. How to pretend that you are not offended in the least while frankly feeling like chewing the carpet! This is the best advice or suggestion I can put forward, the one that *will* make anybody's life a great deal easier. (I find my life very easy as it is, thank you very much!) Someone, a Mr Root, once wrote a very funny and witty book, called, if I remember correctly *Mr Root's Letters* in which he wrote rather abusive letters to all sorts of celebrities and then just published the correspondence which turned out to be very funny and somehow enlightening. One of the funniest exchanges was between a Mr Root and an extremely popular TV presenter at the time, a lady called Esther.

The correspondence started with Mr Root accusing Esther of being incompetent and a waste of time. Back came the reply from Miss Esther thanking Mr Root for his kind comments and wishing him all the very best! Not to be discouraged, Mr Root persisted with more letters to Miss Esther, each more insulting and culminating in calling her a cow or something similar. The more vile his letters, the sweeter came back the replies, complimenting Mr Root and his writing abilities! In the end Mr Root gave up, published a book with this particular correspondence and a few similar ones making a tidy sum in the process. Esther must have had the last laugh though, proving that she had won the epistolary duel and from this I learned that the pleasure of winning is always greater than the fury of an insult, however vile or obscene! As they say, in the end, everybody wins!

Of course, I still occasionally encounter verbal abuse, especially for the way I dress – that is Jermyn Street or Savile Row's best at all times and all occasions; it doesn't matter where I go or what I do, I only wear the best. Of course, the admiring reception I get at Waitrose in King's Road is somehow different from the catcalls and mild insults lavishly spurted on me at Poundland in Brixton. It actually amuses me, I am not afraid of physical attack; I think I could take care of myself, if required, but that is a different story.

I read somewhere that Handel, the great composer, when first coming to London was pelted with stones by people for his sense of dress; Handel wore bright clothes when everyone else was wearing mainly black (they still do to this very day, but a lot less in Chelsea, thank God!). Eventually, Handel was accepted and his music is much loved to this day by the Brits, giving credence to the expression that *The Brits don't much care for music but they love the noise it makes!*

Becoming British

Think of yourself as a newcomer – it helped me in the subtle work of integration more than anything else. Look at me: I came as a refugee, quickly metamorphosed myself into a newcomer and a few years later I was privileged to become a British Citizen. Three easy steps, helped in great measure by Merry who had her own 'interests', and a great deal of other people simply for altruistic reasons and some because they 'liked me'! How strange this country is I thought at the time, but I quickly learned, mainly to my benefit, that there was 'method in their weird habits' to paraphrase the Bard – see how much progress I've made!

Of course, we live in a very diverse world and there is such a multitude of various attitudes, too many to count. Even today, after forty years of being British, I overhear rude comments about 'bloody immigrants' but now I know how to smile politely and point out in passing if given the chance, how the immigrants of previous centuries, the likes of Saxons and Vikings, were not received with open arms and everlasting gratitude at the best of times! Who would have thought eight hundred years ago that one day we'd be buying the cars and almost everything else they make, to mention just a detail or two.

There is a problem though with my way of thinking. The amount of time available for a 'would be refugee' to adapt and become British has changed dramatically and not to the advantage of the human being. Today, you'll be lucky to have a few months 'to adapt/ integrate/participate'; we live in the fast track lane. Everything from shopping to survival and life-changing events are all compressed in weeks, if that, while human beings have hardly changed in centuries! And on top of everything, for the first time in the history of the world science is falling behind the technology with unforeseen and depressing results, but more about this some other time.

Savile Row

There are three things no money can buy, they say: health is one, dignity is the second and 'class' is the third and obviously the most elusive one, especially for the 'nouveau riche' as the Chelsea lot would say having in mind the new influx of Russian oligarchs and their retinue of 'girlfriends' and hangers on. Over the centuries, Chelsea and other desirable places in London and nearby have seen all sorts of influxes of foreigners with enormous amounts of money, and more importantly, money to spend in the UK, and although they moan continuously about yet another foreign billionaire buying this, that and the other, they are very happy to take the money and wait for the next influx of people with enormous amounts of cash to drop in. No questions asked seems to be the authorities' reaction; "It's just not done old boy, just ignore it."!

In 1975, when I was a rare new arrival in Chelsea, absolutely penniless but everybody treated me nicely and fair, the influx of Arab sheiks from the oil-producing countries in the Gulf was in full flow. They came; they spent lots and lots of money, bought properties, but very few in Chelsea. Somehow, for whatever reason, they almost all ended up in North London, Hampstead and the like. Amusing to think that there was I being accepted, rather slowly and perhaps a bit grudgingly in Chelsea's best, while those very rich and showy people with no intention of integrating in any shape or form somehow had to move on. And this phenomenon of slowly moving new people on was not done only to the Arabs and the Russians: it was universally applied in a sensible and smooth manner so as almost not to be noticed. I remember a former head of the European Bank, a French gentleman, good friend of the French President, no less bitterly and publicly complaining that he had lived in Chelsea for six months and nobody had invited him to a local dinner party! Oh dear, he was obviously the wrong person for the job, completely unprepared for the realities of living in Chelsea. He did resign his post eventually!

The following true story makes me smile (laugh actually). All my efforts of integrating seemed to have been working pretty well, so much so that I felt I had to pass one more test and then I'd be very satisfied. This was a more personal matter in fact, but now that I'd made 'a bit of money' perhaps it was time to upgrade my wardrobe, trying something *casually smart*, as Merry put it. Actually, her suggestion took me a bit by surprise. I was wearing decent stuff, elegant and sporty, from traditional well established British shops, the likes of Mark and Spencer and sometimes I'd venture into the boutiques, the likes of Armani and Gucci and so on. I felt quite well and proud of my style but I had to take notice of Merry's suggestion. She'd only rarely make personal suggestions and usually she was right.

I asked Ron for advice; he was smartly dressed and he gave me just one tip – the name of his tailor in Savile Row, a very respected and very old firm and in the process I understood why he looked slim at times; it was the cut of his suits more than Ron slimming!

"What about the price?" I asked Ron.

"More or less what you pay for your Italian designer lot," Ron affirmed firmly.

"Are you serious?" I said, without really understanding his meaning.

"Look Michael," Ron sighed, "when you buy let's say some top Italian designer suit, you buy off the peg, that's the reality of it and most likely it's been manufactured in China by someone making a fiver a week. As for being unique, you must be a uniquely naïve to believe it. Each of all the big designers have more shops than Asda, they sell the same stuff at the airports, in shopping malls, summer fairs and so on, so much for your unique experience. True, all their stuff is made with high quality material and they use very skilled cutters but with few exceptions they are all done to a standard and a price that might impress you or people who haven't seen better, as the case may be. On the other hand, should you have a suit made in Savile Row, well that is a completely different story!"

I was not quite convinced, so I brought the most important argument:

"Come on Ron, they are extremely expensive, you cannot deny that."

"No, value for value their clothes are reasonably priced, and don't laugh. Look at the suit I'm wearing today, how long do you think I've had it for?"

"I don't know, three, four months; you change your suits pretty often."

"Sixteen *years* my dear boy, almost seventeen, actually. I haven't had a suit made for three or four years now, which reminds me, I'll have to go for a fitting for my next batch, put a bit of weight on lately. You see, sixteen years old, it looks almost new and stylish. Bear in mind that only shop assistants and spivs wear bright new suits. Go and see my Mr Alexander, he will make you look like a gentleman; you'd be surprised what he can do."

Just to finish the argument with Ron, I did go and see Mr Alexander. Tailors for a couple of centuries at the same address in Savile Row, a firm of tailors with a bit of a reputation for being more in touch with the modern times, whatever that might be. In fairness, it must be said that some of the more important touches of modern attire have their origin in Savile Row old tailoring houses, covered in historical plaques, commemorating some event or another and stating for everyone to see that they are proud suppliers to the highest in the land, literally, and to the passing trade like me. I went in and the surroundings were more like my gentleman's club in St James's down the road, than any shop I'd ever been in before. I expected to see suits hanging on rails, but there was nothing of the sort and mainly to hide my discomfort I promptly stated, rather abruptly,

"I want to buy a suit."

"Sorry Sir," the elderly, silver-haired gentleman half smiled, "we are only doing bespoke. If Sir would consider having a bespoke suit, we'd be glad to oblige."

A rather long pause from me; the simple matter was that at the time I did not know what the word 'bespoke' meant; I had learned by now, however, how to face an awkward situation in an elegant, dignified manner, or so I'd thought. I eventually smiled, looking straight into the old gentleman's eyes. (Smiling and looking a person openly in the eyes always works in England! At least it gets you out of a tight corner!) Then I said:

"In fact, I was thinking of having more than one," after which I expected a show of gratitude or enthusiasm from the old gentleman, but nothing of the sort came. Unperturbed he must have thought that such an action would be very inappropriate and asked if the gentleman (that being me!) would accept to have his measurements taken.

"But of course," I fully recovered. Someone was summoned to take my measurements and proceeded to take all the usual measurements while I and the old gentleman made small talk. When the chap put his tape around my waist, there was a pause and then the old boy said something funny to make me smile which I duly did exactly when my waist was being measured.

"What size are you usually around your waist Sir?" he enquired.

"Well, I am usually 30, at the most 32, if I've had a heavy lunch." I replied.

"I'm afraid you are 34 Sir," he stated with a hardly concealed smile of satisfaction. His trick of relaxing me with a joke when being measured had worked again for the thousandth time, no doubt!

What! I thought, 34 bloody inches around my waist, that just couldn't be – if there is something I'm really good at, it is my vanity about my looks. A vice / pleasure, which I cherish and always practise in a diligent manner. I am still quite proud of my sporty body, whatever the time and weather might throw at it; very muscular, although a bit short by British standards. Why women like tall men so much is something I could never understand, but here I am!

"Now we have to choose the material, Sir," and the old Gentleman proceeded to show me row after row of exquisite material even to an untrained eye like mine. I promptly chose the one with the most striking colours and asked

"Do you think this will suit me?"

The answer was not what I expected.

"If Sir wants to make a statement, then perhaps," the old Gentleman started before I interrupted.

"OK, I understand. Would you please suggest something that would suit me best?" Of course, I understood that what he meant was, 'If Sir wants to make a fool of himself and look like a prat, then perhaps!'

I ended up ordering three suits, one of them in Prince of Wales motifs and two more sporty ones. They would be ready in twelve weeks and I'd have to attend two fitting sessions inbetween at more or less my leisure! And the bill? I paid some in advance and I was presently surprised to see that the amount was actually lower than I'd expected. I also ordered some shirts and bits and pieces essential for a gentleman with a Savile Row tailor. I left the premises in such a good mood and a great deal of satisfaction; without meaning it, I was on my way to getting rid of one of the two nightmares that follow me even now after more than ten years of being in the UK. This particular one was about things that happened in my childhood, something I'd never told anyone, not even Merry; my survival policy was to try and forget everything that had happened in *Oversylvania*. I knew the best way was never to think back, never. Thinking back just re-traumatises you and you will hinder the process of healing – but however hard I tried not to remember, it kept coming back to haunt me and I hated it.

As a child living on my own, helped by gypsies, I was more or less dressed in rags. I remember a particularly cold winter when the holes in my 'shoes' were so big that I was practically walking barefoot in the snow. The only warm place was in school and I was always the first one to arrive and the last one to leave; no wonder I developed a deep liking for reading and studying. During this time it was not the cold and misery that hurt me as much as the laughs and insults for the way I was 'dressed' by the other children, mainly the children of the 'new order', and children can be extremely cruel at the best of times. Eventually someone, a person I didn't know, took pity on me and one day I received a parcel with an old suit and a pair of solid shoes that fitted me well and frankly, that saved my life. It didn't stop the other children laughing at my ill-fitting clothes though, and I cannot forget that!

Three months later, after two highly rewarding fittings, I was 32 inches around the waist after all, I walked out of Alexander's shop in Savile Row impeccably dressed in my 'Prince of Wales' suit and carrying the other two suits in exclusive covers with a discreet Savile Row label. I smiled to myself and said goodbye for good to my childhood nightmare and the rags I wore and those who laughed at me at the time. For one last second I thought of them and wondered where are they now? And I know the answer. Most likely they are all dead and buried, in ill-fitting suits, no doubt!

Inventions

To be an inventor one must have guts, be determined, single minded, a bore most of the time and definitely self-deprecating!

I am an inventor of some sort; the fact that I have written this tells you how successful or otherwise I've been so far! Still, this brings me, modestly, to the real great inventors and true creators of this world.

At the uni I had a professor, a bit weird even by the highest academic standards (bravo!), to whom I give credit for most of my way of thinking, for what it's worth. He was awarded a Nobel Prize as a reward for some breakthrough inventions in the field of applied physics. He was the guy who put the sparkle of inventing in my mind with one of his favourite expressions

"Go and invent something, doesn't matter what, take no notice of what your peers think about it, ignore everything just follow your imagination. Remember that the person who discovered fire was told in no uncertain terms *Who needs it? There is no market demand for such a 'thing'!*"

This simple reasoning and advice sparked something in me, gave me, without exaggeration, the desire to invent; there was nothing about making mankind a better place to live, nothing of the sort. In my fertile imagination I could actually see how fire had been discovered and most importantly, what happened next, in minute detail. Discovering fire must be amongst the greatest discoveries ever, certainly the most important of its time. Unfortunately, there is no record or name for the person who discovered fire; anyway, I am reliably informed, that he or she was told in no uncertain terms, who needs this thing anyway? It will never catch on and besides, it is dangerous, people could get hurt and you have to top it up all the time to keep it going! Pollution objections and others came later in droves! The smarter objectors went straight to the essence of this 'new' discovery (of course a discovery is always 'new', but somehow this escaped even the brightest minds of the time!). The brightest minds of the cave at the time started seriously analysing this rather inconvenient 'new' discovery, eventually producing in record time a sort of 'peer review' which was damning.

After many experiments and lots of 'heated' arguments, they concluded that the flame of this new thing called 'fire' was nothing but hot air and as such was nothing short of a fraud – who would want to trade in hot air anyway? There are no uses for such nonsense was the scientific conclusion reached by fire specialists who had never seen fire before and that was the end of the matter except for someone who stole a cinder of it and gave it for perpetual safe-keeping to some women called vestals and the rest is history, of sorts! If you think this is too far-fetched, have a look at some of the 19th century newspapers, those describing the visit of a certain Dr Roentgen who claimed to have discovered this new thing called 'radioactivity' or 'x-ray' which he was demonstrating in London for a hefty fee. Well, even the Chairman of the Royal Academy of Science, no less, was asking the London Police to arrest this 'charlatan', taking money under false pretences' – as everybody knew that this thing called 'radioactivity' simply did not exist and could not possibly exist! If that was happening in Britain, country of Faraday, Maxwell, Darwin and the like, just try and imagine what the consequences would have been in a less enlightened place! A deeper thought tells me that perhaps having banned radioactivity at 'its birth' would have been a brilliant idea in the long run – we could have done without the horrors of Hiroshima and Nagasaki for a start!

I amuse myself imagining if someone were to discover fire to-day for the first time and I try and visualise the reaction of the most important people in the world today – no not Donald Trump or Putin, someone much more important – that is The Health and Safety Board! They would have kittens and ban it out of hand, no ifs, no buts, and we'd still be living in caves (some people in London still do nowadays anyway!). All in the name of safety! They would be closely followed by Human Resources of course. What? People gathering close together around this thing, fire or whatever you call it, might even touch one another trying to keep warm; we can't have that! With children present, breathing smoke and eating half cooked meat (they had a late night kebab shop in mind, no doubt!)? Has anybody done a proper risk analysis before God forbid we have a big fire and burn down London, for God's sake?

Luckily, fire was discovered before our modern times and it was too late for governments to ban it, otherwise goodbye to warm water and well cooked food. Mind you, in fairness, getting rid of pre-cooked food might not be such a bad idea after all!

And there was the Establishment, you know. Every self-respecting cave had its own Establishment with their own versions of a 'liberal' newspaper, you might still see the first Guardian tablets with the first spelling mistakes at the British Museum today; and they didn't like the idea of fire whatsoever. What is it for? they asked. Well, it will taste better if you keep the bit of brontosaurus flesh over the flame but the Establishment was not so sure about it as it affected their power. (Just imagine, everyone would have access to fire, oh dear! No way!) Believe it or not, we owe the fire surviving to the present times, you'll never guess, to the chefs or cooks or whoever was preparing meals at the time. It is an historical reality that we owe the preservation of fire and some would say, present day civilisation, and our ready-made meals to a pre-historic master chef, someone with a name like Gordon or Jean-Pierre using almost the same language and methods as seen on telly today and, for variety, a kitchen goddess to increase the ratings, sort of a less tarted up Nigella! Now you know who to blame!

Mona Lisa
The True Story of Mona Lisa *(as told to me by someone else!)*

But the world has made great progress. Look at the artistic achievements over the centuries. Some of you might have even heard of Mona Lisa. (You're welcome to Google it; it is a painting if you want a direct link!) Yes, that's the one, the famous painting, that is, before you think about someone you met at the bar the other night, and you'd rather keep quiet about. The Mona Lisa I'm talking about was the wife of an Italian nobleman and she lived about five hundred years ago as everybody, well almost everybody knows! What is less known and has been a closely kept secret, is the true story of the painting and why Mona Lisa was painted in the first place. She was in fact meant to be the first person to advertise the latest achievements in dentistry – implants. Some smart Florentine dentist came up with the idea, but it was hard to sell it to the fellow Florentines, lack of anaesthetic, undiscovered yet at that time put a spanner in the works, and dentists were also barbers and ironmongers as a rule, now that's multitasking for you. Mind you, some dentists still do that today! So this smart dentist thought publicity, completely unknown at the time, word of mouth was considered good enough – so not much change there! The dentist even invented the word 'publicity' but forgot to claim the copyright for it. Publicity was the way to make implants a success. The idea was to have a 'before' and an 'after' painting of a young lady with almost no teeth looking dejected and modestly dressed in black trying desperately to smile but ashamed to disclose a toothless mouth and most likely, her halitosis as well; her misery being emphasised (you see I can do complex words … just a few!), by a set of ill-fitting second-hand clothes, in a style like let's call it, CHARITY casual! That was to represent 'before', and Leonardo da Vinci (the painter and sculptor and almost everything else) was also commissioned to do a second painting showing the same lady with her mouth full of shining teeth all resting on perfect implants; the lady would also wear the shiniest diamond earrings and the latest fashion from Prada. Striking change, a bit like the transformation from a modest young girl stacking shelves in the supermarket (before) into a fully-fledged footballer's wag (after)! All is fair in war and publicity campaigns!

Unfortunately, the project encountered all sorts of problems, the main one being that no self-respecting Florentine woman would ever agree to be painted toothless so, eventually, Leonardo da Vinci had to settle for the time being for an unfinished portrait which greatly displeased the dentist. As happens in 99% of publicity projects everything ended up in acrimony and claims for compensation. As for who the rightful owner of the painting was, completed or not, that was debatable up until the present day but as the French have it, there is little chance of anything changing soon!

The Mona Lisa painting is still unfinished, the subject hardly known and the contract confusing; the case for compensation has been going through the courts for centuries, justice and its servants taking their time. Eventually, The Supreme Court brought the story to some sort of ending and in a milestone ruling by eight to three, decided in their wisdom that this was a 'run of the mill' painting anyway; who would want to have it? Let the French have it then and the problem would disappear, while they talked it to death! Wise judgement indeed!

VERA
Energy of Time

Reality might be iffy but my dreams are perfect every time. One day I woke up very early in the morning and I saw everything in the clearest light; the same as I'd dreamt it in the night. I went to my desk and I wrote without interruption or correction the following:

The supreme energy, the energy that drives the Universe and everything else is The Energy of Time or VERA as I shall call it.

My theory, the theory of the *Energy of Time* **tries** to explain how the universe and 'everything else' works: the principle that governs the universe. This does not imply lack of modesty on my behalf, but obviously knowledge is knowledge is knowledge and important knowledge is above false modesty. It also does not imply disdain or disregard for many scientists, most of them are brilliant but they are just as brilliant as required by their accepted system, after all, for all I know there might have been brilliant scientists in Atlantis but it made little difference in the end as they could not foresee the future circumstances or do anything about them. As for the question who gave me the right to state my theory as the supreme theory, well, it is the same authority that gave the Wright brothers the right to fly (I somehow don't think they had a pilot's license issued to them before they were 'allowed' the first flight! I am, in short, authorised by the very *Energy of Time*.

Here are the essentials, an ignorant's guide to the *Energy of Time* (or VERA for short.)

Thus Rule I, The Energy of Time

1. Something is moving the universe (and it is not just the inertia from the last Big Bang; some galaxies are actually accelerating).

2. The power moving the universe is preset, impossible to modify, move or affect in any other way; but could eventually be 'tapped into' for all our energy needs.

3. What we euphemistically call TIME is a superficial and frankly primitive understanding of the universe and its forces. The fact that the best brains at present are unanimous (more or less), proves nothing – one can easily visualise conclaves of the best minds in early Middle Ages generally agreeing that the earth was flat, perhaps a bit curiously shaped at the edges, but flat all the same – that was what the evidence of the day concluded. Wind up to the present day and replace flat earth with the theory of relativity, and you could put the equal sign between the two!

4. It is not the movement of the planets or stars that matters; if all planets move tomorrow, you and I and everybody else will age all the same, irrespective of how we measure it! – but VERA is the force that moves the stars and planets and everything else. (Too often we confuse actuality with reality.) From the movement of the electron to the expansion of the biggest galaxy, there is an energy behind it. The *Energy of Time* or VERA as I call it for short. The planets and everything else are energised by VERA according to size and density.

5. Our laws of physics are fundamentally flaws based on the principle that we can not have energy without mass ($e=mc^2$ and the like, particles and all, but there is life beyond particles, something that moves the particles, as a matter of fact *there* is where the *Energy of Time* resides). As the universe is made mainly of **dark matter,** and obviously outside our perceptions and definitions of mass and certainly with a great deal of energy (it moves everything after all!), **our accepted universal laws** are more similar to local Parish by-laws than the **REAL** universal laws of almost everything.

(Add the String theories for good measure and a good laugh!)

6. Unfortunately, in the middle of the 19th century we discovered electromagnetism and then nuclear energy with the net result that now we have mobile phones and nuclear weapons but we produce energy by burning stuff (just slightly more efficient than our Neanderthal ancestors in their favourite caves). To say that electromagnetism is on a par with gravity is frankly bizarre at best and barmy at worst. How amusing to see top physicists ('top' as described by themselves and their cohorts), stating that 'gravity is a very weak force'! That is about the power that holds the universe together, while nuclear energy, particles moving and everything electromagnetic are phenomenally powerful! Perhaps someone should tell them that all electromagnetic powers in the world put together could not defy the slightest form of gravity. Billions and billions of phenomenally powerful nuclear explosions take place every nanosecond in the universe without affecting its gravity in the slightest.

7. Gravity is the force that holds the universe together, through its gravitational waves we have the speed of infinity. VERA is the energy that powers the universe and its waves have also the speed of infinity.

8. To express what really happens with the universe (and by the way it is only one universe, never mind the fancy theories), The *Energy of Time* is the driving energy while gravity holds the universe together with all its continuous changes and loose formats and the like. **These two are the supreme energies, everything else is subordinated to their powers.**

9. Finally, just imagine that there is a way of tapping into the energy that moves the universe and the repercussions of having free unlimited energy anywhere on earth or space,

anywhere where time exists! And time (the *Energy of Time*) exists everywhere from the smallest particles to almighty galaxies.

The Energy of Time is the supreme form of energy. Any other form of energy can be affected, moved, applied deliberately if we want, destroyed even, but nothing touches the *Energy of Time* but itself.

* * *

That was my final manifesto before going to real work in 1991 and doing what I should have done fifteen years earlier. The aim was now clearly defined and the milestones were set in stone. After having the moment of rage against myself for wasting so much time, (ironic, isn't it?) I started doing my long delayed real work.

I spent over ten years trying to convince completely disinterested people and dismissive ones too, about my *Energy of Time*. I wrote to almost every oil and gas company, all major banks and every scientific institution I could think of – all a total and complete waste of effort and I must admit that at times I was overwhelmed by sheer desperation, but somehow I always managed to pull myself through. The following little happening helped me a great deal and radically changed my way of thinking.

I was on a train late for an interview, I needed that particular temporary job desperately, my income being next to non-existent at that time, time to show everybody how brilliant I was, just have a look at my *Energy of Time*. And the train was late, it was going to be too late for my interview and I was fuming with despair, actually cursing the blasted train and everything else when from one station a new passenger joined the carriage. It was a young woman with her severely disabled young child in some sort of oversized pram. The child was crying continuously, shouting with violent spasms of movement which the young woman tended to with care and a kind and open smile. She had that kind smile of love for her child that I've only seen in Britain, and I could never really explain. Instinctively I compared myself to this woman who was 'sentenced' to a very difficult life with her severely disabled child and she was facing it with a kind smile while I, I was nothing but some sort of fraud, upset that the train was late, that I wouldn't get a poncey job working for idiots most probably and worried that I might not be able to afford expensive wines or whatever anymore. How pathetic! I left the train and went straight back home and destroyed every letter I had meant to send to everybody. The time for real work had arrived.

Time for experimental work, and this did not start well at all. I spent another three years trying to 'control' the *Energy of Time*, such a wild goose chase that I'm embarrassed. I spent every single penny I had left, then whatever I got from my temporary work, in trying to create devices to 'control' the *Energy of Time*; an absurd venture by any standards but somehow I did not see it at that time. I kept telling myself 'remember, you are British, fight and fight again, otherwise you should never have come to Britain, you should have stayed in your poncey *Oversylvania* feeling sorry for yourself! Thinking back to *Oversylvania* was an extremely rare occurrence for me; my rule was that thinking back meant to be re-traumatised which was the last thing I wanted to indulge myself in! It dawned on me eventually that trying to control the uncontrollable was impossible, however smart I thought I was. Control it with what? There was nothing to control with the energy that powers the universe.

What next then, because there was a very interesting 'next'? What about tapping into this marvellous infinite energy for our daily needs? That would not only prove that I had been right all along (more or less!), but it would also solve mankind's greatest requirements, the ever-increasing thirst for energy. If I could work out a device that tapped into the waves of the *Energy of Time*, then all I had to do was to convert it into electricity for instance! That would mean of course the end of the tyranny of oil; it would also mean free energy for everyone all over the world – I couldn't see anyone, even the most determined and ruthless dictator, being able to mess up with the *Energy of Time*. Of course, most of the big companies would disappear or adapt, the economic changes would be staggering and the impetus in mankind's development phenomenal. It would be a bigger change than the last jump, from steam to electromagnetism. Of course, other ways of tapping into the *Energy of Time* would be discovered by others, but I was the standard-bearer of this extraordinary transformation!

* * *

First working device

By the end of 2010, fourteen years after my first attempt to get a patent for VERA, the *Energy of Time*, promptly refused by the powers that be, I started the practical work of devising a small device in which I could 'trap' a certain size of wave from VERA and convert it through a series of 'time (VERA) mirrors' into movement and the movement into electricity – electricity for free for everybody everywhere, no less! Meanwhile, I had already devised a system of measuring standards for VERA; for instance One Teng = the Energy required for one earth rotation, as an example. I published a little booklet, describing, in practical terms, the principle of my device, without divulging how it actually works and definitely not what the VERA mirrors were made of or how they work – the essence of the device! I actually published the functioning sketch of my device but I did not divulge the 'commercial aspects' and overall, I was terribly proud of it.

Of course, I still needed funds to buy the most elementary bits of equipment and as luck would have I got some very juicy contracts from various oil and gas companies during this period, which I found hilarious – my device when fully functional and mass produced would put these very companies out of business almost overnight! What a mixed bunch they were – they *are* – the same cheating, lying, jostling for position being the rules of the game but much worse; more competition, more criminality seems now to be the rule of the day! Still, they paid unknowingly for my tools and instruments and slowly, slowly my device started to take form.

First, I thought, I'd do it in the shape of a battery, batteries were more and more in demand, but the chemicals and other materials for the actual battery were hard to procure and unstable. Not to worry, I remembered that once at uni, I'd observed an experiment in which a ray of light was 'killed'; it had been done by directing a ray of light bouncing into a system of mirrors set at certain angles, each of the mirrors slightly darker than the previous one until the last mirror which was totally black, where the light 'died'. Of course, the light disappeared but what happened to the energy of light, that could not disappear? Energy always transforms, never disappears; thus goes the 'universal law'! Discuss!

But this gave me the best idea for my device. I would use the same 'bouncing wave principle' but instead of a ray of light I would use a 'ray' of VERA. All was ready for building the real prototype when things started turning nasty. All my temporary jobs that kept the project going disappeared over night, and I had not even been asked for an interview after applying for literally hundreds of jobs – it was like someone had drawn a curtain on my name with the notice ***Do not touch under any circumstances***.

Other things happened to, unpleasant things designed to make my life as uncomfortable as possible. I knew that most companies operated secretly a list of 'troublemakers', not to be employed, mainly trade union or Labour party people. I knew of its existence, I'd even had a glimpse at it many years previously – it was a very well codified and innocent looking list, and as such could escape the hackers' attention! I knew that being on that list meant you'd never work again, except for yourself. At that time I had a very strong feeling that I must be on the dreaded list. Then a very good job was offered to me, in Switzerland of all places, working for a Swiss firm, which I later found out was a 'front' for a Russian conglomerate – the whole set-up being a ruse to by-pass sanctions imposed on Russia for the Crimea annexation. However, I needed money desperately and I jumped at the prospect, especially as they paid me some money in advance.

I arrived in Zurich, I was put in a comfortable hotel and started work straightaway on a very improbable project control system. I did my best, I went around Zurich countryside at the weekend and everything was nice and pleasant. Too nice and too pleasant for my liking! One of the conditions of my new job was that I used my own laptop and it wasn't long before someone in the office tried to hack into it.

In London, somewhere, I have a laptop that has never been connected to a power plug even, never connected to the internet, bought second-hand with the modem removed and camera and sound disabled – it has never left the secure place in my flat! When I enter my password I always put a black cover over the keyboard; a little advice for those using their laptop in any public place, con-ference hall and the like – bear in mind that there is always a cam-era or a mirror above you which will see your password however complex you make it. All hackers' greatest desire is to have a mirror above your keyboard when you enter your password! 95% of all hacking is done this way!

My trip to Zurich turned out to be a great deal shorter than I expected. After two of my Russian 'colleagues' physically broke into my laptop when I was in an arranged 'meeting', and removed the C drive, it was clear that my job was not exactly what it had said in the job description. To cut a long story short, the same after-noon someone hit me hard on the head and pushed me from the third floor down the stairs – luck alone saved my life and I went straight back to London happy to be in one piece, couple of black eyes only, and leaving the 'job', laptop and money in my office desk, never to be seen again. I also hope not to see the Russian lot again, either!

Back in London my life took a rather bad turn. On average I would get about five or six letters a day, but for weeks I'd not been getting any communications of any sort, not even adverts for pizza delivery! To cut a long story short, it was clear that someone was 'after me'; in a way I was relieved – at last someone was taking me and my *Energy of Time* seriously, but whoever that person was, they were not necessarily going to be friendly. I converted a little mobile radio into a 'bug finder unit', easy to do and very cheap, with the net result of finding eighteen listening and visual devices within half an hour. I left them all in place; they would only have been replaced by better hidden ones.

I had to take 'defensive action'; at that time my system was producing one millionth of a volt in electricity, an extremely tiny amount, but it was coming directly from VERA.

It was the first time that anyone had tapped into the *Energy of Time*!

The day the first experiment worked I had a strange reaction. OK, it worked, but I'd always known it would work, so my elation was more directed towards those who had laughed me out of court and had ridiculed my discovery and now this extraordinary invention. Modestly, I could say 'this *will* solve all energy needs for propelling mankind into the next phase of development', but I dearly wanted to go to Imperial, to Cambridge – no, not Oxford, too stupid for words! – and say in a modest manner, "Obviously, I told you so, my dear Sir. You never believed me, you ridiculed me and my work, but here it is!"

Still, there were more important things to be done, before somebody stole my invention, or worse! I thought the best thing to do would be to hide the device for the time being, just till things cooled off and the people so interested now, became less interested. Perhaps if I started behaving in a more bizarre manner and make some outlandish statements, that would convince the interested parties that I was just a lunatic and better ignored. That would give me the chance to live and carry on my work on the quiet!

Meanwhile, I split my VERA device into two parts and hid one part in one of London's oldest graveyards while I sent the other part abroad, through someone I could trust. Margaret, who had a vague idea of what I was doing, undertook to go to a certain place in *Oversylvania*, taking the other part with her, mainly the VERA mirrors, to be buried in a very quiet place. One part could not function without the other part and unless set up properly first time, the device would self-destruct. I am the only person who knows how to set it up properly first time, only I.

* * *

Life and the Energy of Time

Something that attracts attention from some circles is my explanation of life in relation to the *Energy of Time* (VERA).

Most of the properties attributed to living systems can be found in non-living systems too, clouds 'grow', crystals reproduce, metals 'react' and so on. For those interested there are libraries written about life 'characteristics' (its complexity, uniqueness, holism, evolution, unpredictability, teleology, and others). However, one stands out, the one called *'vitalism'*, which goes on the principle that life cannot be explained by ordinary physical laws as known until now (a very correct assumption) and as such there should be an extra constituent, a life force which infuses every single biological system and that accounts for the exceptional powers and capabilities. Yes, there is a life force, an *'elan vital'* and that is the atoms revolt against Veraias (demi-waves of the *Energy of Time*). This rebellious behaviour, when atoms are trying to and succeeding in disobeying the behaviour as ordained by Veraias, leads the molecules to conform to a global 'master plan' the energy of which is furnished by the Veraias themselves. It is also true that as the molecules develop the 'mechanistic' theory of life comes into action, but that is only after the life has been established, and at no time excludes the *'elan vital'*, it merely complements it. It is the mechanism through which life builds and expands but it is not life itself. No amount of mechanistic theory will ever explain why anything alive 'wants desperately to live as long as possible (the curious 'exceptions' like the lemmings are just fairy tales, the lemmings do not know they are going to die), and it is that that enables a 'brainless' virus to disguise as something else.

As we shall see later my theory shows that the *Energy of Time* moves in an ever expanding quasi-circle in a way that can be best described as a track race where, if we take the start point as the **previous** Big Bang where the *Energy of Time* re-started from, it will race with various speeds on the uniform, quasi-circular track, without actually completely leaving the start line. When the racing *Energy of Time* reaches again the initial start line it will overlap the original *Energy of Time* which has not left one lap behind and the collision will produce the next Big Bang. We all know about Nemesis and his theory that we all will live again with the same friends and fellow citizens and that we'll all go through the same experience and same activities, which is a fascinating theory and true in the statement 'that the restoration of the universe takes place not once but again and again and again in all eternities.' Correct. The 'restoration' of a universe is true but there will be a different universe every time.

What is Life?

I'd better explain! For a start this is a lovely question and as for all lovely things there seems to be no apparent answer. The point I must stress here is that as far as Life is concerned, it is subjected to a double influence of VERA (the *Energy of Time*). One is the effect of the 'internal Veraias' present in every particle within a living organism and the effect of the *Enveloping Energy of Time* which ends up by always putting an end to the very life.

Life is the phenomenon that takes place when and where the particles 'revolt' against the strands of *Energy of Time*. It is not viruses or disease or accidents or violence that kills life, finishes off a life, but the very *Energy of Time* that does it. Viruses, diseases and all the rest are nothing but the tools used by the *Energy of Time* (VERA).

Is there life in any other part of the universe? No, definitely not in the form we are. By its own nature the *Energy of Time* could allow only one form of uprising, after all, true 'revolutionaries' are unique!

Although it will logically follow that the more complex living organisms become, the more adaptable at 'revolting' they are and generally they are; but even the most sophisticated human behaviour is nothing short of 'trying to cheat' the *Energy of Time*. On the 'highest' scale it is not survival only that counts but the most comfortable, satisfying survival too! But sophisticated attempts of cheating the *Energy of Time* could be found in very 'primitive' organisms. I use the word 'primitive' in its more wide acceptance, because as far as VERA is concerned there is nothing primitive about a virus that disguises itself better and more efficiently than any human can do (as we can see in the case of cancer for instance).

In the order of things, it is pretty safe to assume that it is not the 'fittest' that survives longer but the most adaptable; the biggest 'cheat' is the one that survives longest; the species that manages to fool the *Energy of Time* for a certain period is the one that will live to procreate, but in the end it is not the species with the stronger genes that survive, but those with the most adaptable genes. There is no doubt that the dinosaurs had perfectly strong genes, (20 million years have proved just that!) but where are they now? While the insects with rather dodgy genes are quietly 'running' the earth ever since.

The continuous 'struggle' between life and the VERA, its unpredictable relationship makes life itself unpredictable and that is in a sense the very huge diversity and the very beauty of it. Identifying Veraias would make us understand the process of life, the very sequence of events in the same manner as genes identify certain aspects of the organisms.

Life from its most 'primitive' forms to us is the only 'thing' in the universe where matter refuses to accept its status that of what it was meant to be. Rebellion is not the exclusive prerogative of the human race (or at least some of the human race!) as some philosophers would have us believe. The appearance of life itself is the ultimate act of rebellion against the very *Energy of Time*. The fact that this particularly supreme form of rebellion ends up inevitably in defeat is hardly a reason for despair. After all, high jump competitions always end in defeat but we are still happily competing! We know we are going to die eventually but we 'have a go' at life.

* * *

On practical terms my life has been the best I could have imagined, and even more if that were possible. I came to Britain when I was twenty-two, I've spent all my working life in these amazing surroundings, I encounter the highest emotions, I have met the most interesting characters but most importantly I became British! – Officially (with passport to prove it) and, humanly, if that is the correct word! In true local tradition I have tried to do my best, sometimes blowing my own trumpet a bit too much! (I'm the first one to admit.) I have seen more beauty than perhaps one ought to be entitled to. I have lived among people who have made me understand what being tolerant means, what fairness is all about –

and if they ever re-design the Union Jack, they should write on it the words *Tolerance, Fairness* and *Class*. It is true for all to see!

Furthermore, I'd add the word kindness, in all its aspects, from the smallest gesture to the final sacrifice; I will forget many things but never the British kindness that I encounter almost daily. As for Chelsea, the best way to encapsulate the very essence of the place is the small gesture I once saw around Cheney Walk; an old lady had lost her pet, a cat, and in typical Chelsea fashion she'd taken to writing and placing little posters on trees with the cat's photograph and offering a reward for the return of the wandering tabby! Nothing out of the ordinary in that, but after recovering her pet, who had returned under his own steam, the old lady replaced the old posters with new ones which were in effect a thank you letter addressed to all those who had helped her and her cat. This could only happen in Chelsea!

Still, as I need some money for an alternative prototype, I've come upon an idea how to alleviate this particular necessity. I will start selling *The Big Issue,* a publication to help the poor and the unemployed … from tomorrow. I shall be the oldest person doing it, but age is not an impediment to me, and I shall dress nicely and try to look my best. I shall have to sell quite a few copies, so I can carry on working on my second prototype, and still have something left for food.

I haven't chosen my patch yet, it is to be either in front of M&S or Waitrose, in King's Road – Chelsea of course!

Final

I, the Undersigned, bequeath all my possessions, including the prototype for VERA (the *Energy of Time*), with all its relevant documentation, to the British Nation; all British people and their pets, as my thank you for their kindness and fairness. All and every one of them!

I was born crying but I shall die with the widest smile!

The End